Paul's Letter to the Romans

Paul's Letter to the Romans

Thomas D. Stegman, SJ
with Little Rock Scripture Study staff

Little Rock Scripture Study

LITURGICAL PRESS
Collegeville, Minnesota

littlerockscripture.org

Nihil obstat: Reverend Robert Harren, *Censor librorum.*
Imprimatur: ✠ Most Reverend Patrick M. Neary, C.S.C., Bishop of St. Cloud, Minnesota, April 29, 2026.

Cover design by John Vineyard. Interior art by Ned Bustard.

This symbol indicates material that was created by Little Rock Scripture Study to supplement the biblical text and commentary. Some of these inserts first appeared in the *Little Rock Catholic Study Bible*; others were created specifically for this book by Amy Ekeh.

Library of Congress Cataloging-in-Publication Data

Names: Stegman, Thomas author | Little Rock Scripture Study Staff author
Title: Paul's letter to the Romans / Thomas D. Stegman, SJ, with Little Rock Scripture Study staff.
Description: Collegeville, MN : Liturgical Press, [2026] | Series: Little Rock scripture study | Summary: "This study explores Paul's Letter to the Romans and the themes that are most essential to Christian life: faith, salvation, relationships, and community. Commentary, study and reflection questions, prayers, and access to online lectures are included. 6 lessons"—Provided by publisher.
Identifiers: LCCN 2026018005 | ISBN 9780814665350 trade paperback | ISBN 9780814665114 epub
Subjects: LCSH: Bible. Romans | Christian life—Biblical teaching | BISAC: RELIGION / Biblical Studies / New Testament / Paul's Letters | RELIGION / Biblical Commentary / New Testament / Paul's Letters | LCGFT: Commentaries
Classification: LCC BS2665.6.C48 S74 2026
LC record available at https://lccn.loc.gov/2026018005

TABLE OF CONTENTS

Welcome 7

What materials will you use? 8

How will you use these materials? 8

Preface 11

Lesson One (Introduction and Romans 1:1–3:20) 13

Lesson Two (Romans 3:21–5:21) 31

Lesson Three (Romans 6–8) 47

Lesson Four (Romans 9–11) 61

Lesson Five (Romans 12:1–15:13) 77

Lesson Six (Romans 15:14–16:27) 93

Praying with Your Group 107

Reflecting on Scripture 109

Wrap-Up Lectures and Discussion Tips for Facilitators are available for each lesson at no charge. Find them online at LittleRockScripture.org/Lectures/Romans.

Welcome

The Bible is at the heart of what it means to be a Christian. It is the Spirit-inspired word of God for us. It reveals to us the God who created, redeemed, and guides us still. It speaks to us personally and as a church. It forms the basis of our public liturgical life and our private prayer lives. It urges us to live worthily and justly, to love tenderly and wholeheartedly, and to be a part of building God's kingdom here on earth.

Though it was written a long time ago, in the context of a very different culture, the Bible is no relic of the past. Catholic biblical scholarship is among the best in the world, and in our time and place, we have unprecedented access to it. By making use of solid scholarship, we can discover much about the ancient culture and religious practices that shaped those who wrote the various books of the Bible. With these insights, and by praying with the words of Scripture, we allow the words and images to shape us as disciples. By sharing our journey of faithful listening to God's word with others, we have the opportunity to be stretched in our understanding and to form communities of love and learning. Ultimately, studying and praying with God's word deepens our relationship with Christ.

Paul's Letter to the Romans

The resource you hold in your hands is divided into six lessons. Each lesson involves personal prayer and study using this book and the experience of group prayer, discussion, and wrap-up lecture.

If you are using this resource in the context of a small group, we suggest that you meet six times, discussing one lesson per meeting. Allow about 90 minutes for the small group gathering. Small groups function best with eight to twelve people to ensure good group dynamics and to allow all to participate as they wish.

Some groups choose to have an initial gathering before their regular sessions begin. This allows an opportunity to meet one another, pass out books, and, if desired, view the optional introductory lecture for this study available on the "Resources" page of the Little Rock Scripture Study website (LittleRockScripture.org). Please note that there is only one introductory lecture for two-part studies.

Every Bible study group is a little bit different. Some of our groups like to break each lesson up into two weeks of study so they are reading less each week and have more time to discuss the questions together at their weekly gatherings. If your group wishes to do this, simply agree how much of each lesson will be read each week, and only answer the questions that correspond to the material you read. Wrap-up lectures can then be viewed at the end of every other meeting rather than at the end of every meeting. Of course, this will mean that your study will last longer, and your group will meet more times.

WHAT MATERIALS WILL YOU USE?

The materials in this book include:

- The text of Romans, using the New American Bible, Revised Edition as the translation.
- Commentary by Thomas D. Stegman, SJ.
- Occasional inserts highlighting elements of the chapters of Romans being studied. Some of these appear also in the *Little Rock Catholic Study Bible* while others are supplied by staff writers.
- Questions for study, reflection, and discussion at the end of each lesson.
- Opening and closing prayers for each lesson, as well as other prayer forms available in the closing pages of the book.

In addition, there are wrap-up lectures available for each lesson. Your group may choose to purchase a DVD containing these lectures or make use of the video lectures available online at no charge. The link to these free lectures is: LittleRockScripture.org/Lectures/Romans. Of course, if your group has access to qualified speakers, you may choose to have live presentations.

Each person will need a current translation of the Bible. We recommend the *Little Rock Catholic Study Bible*, which makes use of the New American Bible, Revised Edition. Other translations, such as the New Jerusalem Bible or the New Revised Standard Version: Catholic Edition, would also work well.

HOW WILL YOU USE THESE MATERIALS?

Prepare in advance

Using Lesson One as an example:

- Begin with a simple prayer like the one found on page 13.
- Read the assigned material for Lesson One (pages 14–26) so that you are prepared for the weekly small group session.

- Answer the questions, Exploring Lesson One, found at the end of the assigned reading, pages 27–29.
- Use the Closing Prayer on page 30 when you complete your study. This prayer may be used again when you meet with the group.

Meet with your small group

- After introductions and greetings, allow time for prayer (about 5 minutes) as you begin the group session. You may use the prayer on page 13 (also used by individuals in their preparation) or use a prayer of your choosing.
- Spend about 45–50 minutes discussing the responses to the questions that were prepared in advance. You may also develop your discussion further by responding to questions and interests that arise during the discussion and faith-sharing itself.
- Close the discussion and faith-sharing with prayer, about 5–10 minutes. You may use the Closing Prayer at the end of each lesson or one of your choosing at the end of the book. It is important to allow people to pray for personal and community needs and to give thanks for how God is moving in your lives.
- View the wrap-up lecture associated with each lesson (12–15 minutes). You may watch the lecture online, use a DVD, or provide a live lecture by a qualified local speaker. View the lecture together at the end of the session or, if your group runs out of time, you may invite group members to watch the lecture on their own time after the discussion.

A note to individuals

- If you are using this resource for individual study, simply move at your own pace. Take as much time as you need to read, study, and pray with the material.
- If you would like to share this experience with others, consider inviting a friend or family member to join you for your next study. Even a small group of two or three provides an opportunity for fruitful dialog and faith-sharing!

PREFACE

Welcome to *Paul's Letter to the Romans*! I'd like to share a story with you about how this study came to be.

Fr. Tom Stegman, SJ, the author of your study, was a New Testament scholar and beloved professor who served for some years as dean of the Clough School of Theology and Ministry at Boston College. Fr. Stegman's expertise in Paul's letters was well-known. His enthusiasm for them was legendary. He thrived on helping others break open the rich treasury of Paul's letters and come to a fuller understanding of the life-changing reality of the death and resurrection of Jesus.

In 2019, Fr. Stegman was diagnosed with glioblastoma, an aggressive form of brain cancer. Over the next four years, Fr. Stegman's Jesuit formation, personal determination, lively sense of humor, and steadfast faith served him well as he wrestled with cancer and its debilitating effects.

Fr. Stegman loved to work, and he did not stop working until the very end. In 2022, he retired from Boston College and moved to Campion Center, which serves as home for Jesuits in need of specialized medical care. It was Fr. Stegman's wish to spend his time at Campion praying and writing.

And write he did. It was at Campion that Fr. Stegman wrote this commentary. He was so excited to dig into the project that as he waited for a desk to be moved into his room, he began working on it while sitting in bed with a computer on his lap! In the following months, typing errors became a common frustration as Fr. Stegman's illness progressed and certain mechanical tasks became increasingly difficult. "I can fix the typos," I told him. "Just write about Romans." It was clear that—typos aside—he was still writing beautiful commentary. He was still preaching the gospel.

Fr. Stegman loved St. Paul, and he loved Paul's Letter to the Romans. Some of his final days among us were spent pouring himself into the commentary you'll soon be reading. As you read Fr. Stegman's words alongside those of St. Paul, it is my prayer that both of these faithful men may bless you and lead you to a fuller understanding of the love of God in Christ Jesus, a love that has been poured into our hearts and from which nothing—neither death nor life nor any other thing—can separate us.

Amy Ekeh, Editor

The World of Paul

Paul's Letter to the Romans

LESSON ONE

Introduction and Romans 1:1–3:20

Begin your personal study and group discussion with a simple and sincere prayer such as:

Prayer

Loving God, send your Spirit upon us as we study the writings of your apostle Paul. Open our ears, our minds, and especially our hearts. Deepen your love within us, and transform us to embody and proclaim the good news you have revealed in your son Jesus Christ.

Read the Introduction on pages 14–16 and the Bible text of Romans 1:1–3:20, found in the outside columns of pages 17–26, highlighting what stands out to you.

Read the accompanying commentary to add to your understanding.

Respond to the questions on pages 27–29, Exploring Lesson One.

The Closing Prayer on page 30 is for your personal use and may be used at the end of group discussion.

INTRODUCTION

We are about to embark on a study of Paul's Letter to the Romans. This letter has been the subject of much of my teaching and research as a Scripture scholar for two main reasons. First, as part of the canon of the New Testament, this letter is not only *Paul's* word to the church in Rome, written nearly two thousand years ago; we also believe it is *God's* word directed to us. Indeed, and second, I find in this letter a great deal that applies to us now—as individuals, as members of the church, and as citizens. In Romans, Paul takes up topics that have an uncanny relevance today, such as:

- his emphasis on the importance of God's work of reconciliation and how the church should embody this reconciliation;
- his teaching about the transforming power of the Holy Spirit and how the Spirit assists us in prayer (in fact, the most extended treatment of the Spirit in the New Testament is found in Romans);
- his exhortations to the Roman Christians about how to resolve differences among them;
- his teaching about what constitutes true freedom; and his understanding of the effects of baptism.

In addition, Romans contains a depth of material about God and God's covenant faithfulness that is grounded in love. This divine love is revealed through Jesus, who:

- as God's Son and the Messiah (Christ), does what only God can do in bringing about our salvation: restores right relationship with God and one another;
- as the new Adam, reveals what authentic human living entails; and
- shows forth the richness of what salvation is and what it calls forth from us.

As you can see, these topics are both wide-ranging and life-changing. Paul has much to say to us about the things that are most essential to Christian life: faith, salvation, relationships, and community.

Before looking closely at the text of the letter, it will be helpful for us to examine some preliminary issues.

AUTHORSHIP AND DATE

The New Testament contains thirteen letters attributed to Paul's authorship. Many scholars question whether all of them were produced by the apostle himself during his lifetime, but nobody doubts that the Letter to the Romans is from Paul—although it was penned by a secretary named Tertius (16:22). Romans is Paul's longest and one of his latest letters, written after his ministry and letters to the Galatians and Corinthians. In fact, the issues with which he dealt in those letters (e.g., the primacy of faith, the nature of life in the Spirit, and the need to strive for unity in the Christian community) are set forth in Romans in an amplified manner. That is, in Romans we're receiving Paul's mature teaching on these important themes. Given what we know about Paul's life and ministry, a good guess is that this letter was written in the late 50s CE.

AUDIENCE

Unlike most of Paul's letters, Romans was written to a church that Paul as a missionary had not founded. It is not clear when the gospel, or "good news," first came to the capital of the empire. Most scholars surmise that it was Jewish Christian missionaries who first proclaimed the good news in Rome. What we do know is that the Christians in Rome, at the time of Paul's writing, consisted of both Jewish and Gentile believers, and that they met in separate house churches. In all probability, these house churches formed along ethnic lines.

In the year 49 CE, the emperor Claudius expelled from the city a number of leading Jews, including some members of the Christian community, for civic unrest as they quarreled over whether Jesus was truly the Messiah, God's Son who came to bring salvation. This exile was lifted before Paul wrote the letter. We should imagine a context in which those Jewish Christians who returned found that their Gentile brothers and sisters had taken on new roles in the community, including filling some leadership positions. Thus, there were tensions between the groups, and the apostle learned about these through members of the community whom he knew from prior ministry (16:3-16). These tensions included issues of worship and table fellowship.

PURPOSE IN WRITING

Near the beginning and end of the letter, Paul provides us with important information about his present circumstances and future goals. Paul had already founded churches in cities that ring the Aegean Sea (i.e., in present-day Greece and Turkey). Having established these communities, Paul now wished to turn to the west. As one who was called to proclaim the gospel where it was not yet known (15:20), he wanted to go to Spain, to the westernmost part of the empire. In order to minister there, he knew he would need help—e.g., financial support, assistance from translators, introductions to meet certain persons, and other logistical matters—and he hoped the Roman Christians could provide it.

In order to gain their trust in and support for his ministry, Paul sets forth his proclamation of the gospel. This historical context explains one of the unique features of Romans. Whereas in other letters Paul can allude to and refer back to things he has already taught, here he presents his gospel to the Romans for the first time. Moreover, he sends his co-worker Phoebe ahead of him and asks the Romans to cooperate with her as she tries to get things moving on gathering their assistance (16:1-2). It is likely that Phoebe brought the letter to the community and read it to them. It is also quite possible that she was the first interpreter of the letter, answering questions the Romans may have had when listening to it. (Indeed, it would be surprising if they didn't have questions!)

Paul doesn't only ask for assistance, however. As the apostle sent to the Gentiles (1:5), he also wants to bolster their faith and encourage them. Thus, the letter has a mutual function: Paul and the community need one another, a dynamic that remains true in the church today between ministers and those to whom they minister.

GENRE AND LITERARY CHARACTERISTICS

As we have already observed, Romans is unique in that Paul presents a systematic explanation of the gospel that he regularly proclaims

Features of Greco-Roman letters as found in Romans

Opening greetings	Includes name and title of sender, name of person or community addressed, and a greeting.	Romans 1:1-7
Thanksgiving	Gives thanks to God for a particular reason. (In Greco-Roman letters, sender gives thanks to "the gods.")	Romans 1:8-15
Body of letter	Includes everything between the opening and closing of the letter. Usually begins with a reason for writing, and often ends with a summary of the basic message of the letter.	Romans 1:16–15:13
Conclusion of letter	Often expresses a desire to visit (15:22-33). Includes mutual greetings (16:3-24) and a final blessing (16:25-27).	Romans 15:14–16:27

in his missionary work. But Romans is not simply a theological treatise per se. It is also a real letter containing all the features of a letter from this time: opening greetings, a thanksgiving paragraph, the letter body, mutual greetings near the end, and a final blessing. The best way to describe Romans is that it is a theological essay expressed in letter form.

As such, Romans has certain characteristics to which we should be alert. One is the dialectical quality of Paul's approach, or the way he expresses or explains his ideas. Because the content of the "gospel of God" (1:1)—a reference to the good news about what God has done in sending his Son and the Holy Spirit—is so profound, the apostle takes several steps in setting it forth. In doing so, he refers to earlier material in the letter and intersperses a good deal of explanatory material.

One of the ways Paul explains is through the use of *diatribe*. This term refers to a literary device in which an imaginary interlocutor or conversation partner is allowed to raise questions and even possible objections. These interjections allow Paul to give more precision to his presentation and to clarify possible misunderstandings. As contemporary readers, it will be helpful to understand and anticipate the use of this technique as we read and follow Paul's explanations.

Another notable feature of Romans is Paul's ample use of Scripture. (Note that the Scriptures of Paul and Jesus were what we now call the Hebrew Bible or the Old Testament.) In fact, over half of the Old Testament references in the Pauline corpus are found in Romans. Sometimes Paul cites Scripture directly, while at other times he alludes to it. In citing and alluding to Scripture, Paul presumes that we are familiar with the context of the passages at hand. At times, we will have to pay close attention to this feature.

KEY THEME AND LETTER STRUCTURE

A phrase we will encounter many times in Romans is "the righteousness of God." This phrase refers both to an attribute of God and to the divine activity that emanates from it. In short, it points to God's covenant faithfulness and to the divine commitment to make right what has gone wrong and, in mercy, to restore right relationships between God and human beings, and within the human community itself.

In the six lessons of our study, we will explore how Paul proclaims this theme, following the basic outline of Romans below:

- Address (1:1-15); Humanity Lost Without the Gospel (1:16–3:20)
- Justification Through Faith in Christ (3:21–5:21)
- Justification and the Christian Life (6:1–8:39)
- Jews and Gentiles in God's Plan (9:1–11:36)
- The Duties of Christians (12:1–15:13)
- Conclusion (15:14–16:27)

I: Address

CHAPTER 1

Greeting

[1]Paul, a slave of Christ Jesus, called to be an apostle and set apart for the gospel of God, [2]which he promised previously through his prophets in the holy scriptures, [3]the gospel about his Son, descended from David according to the flesh, [4]but established as Son of God in power according to the spirit of holiness through resurrection from the dead, Jesus Christ our Lord. [5]Through him we have received the grace of apostleship, to bring about the obedience of faith, for the sake of his name, among all the Gentiles, [6]among whom are you also, who are called to belong to Jesus Christ; [7]to all the beloved of God in Rome, called to be holy. Grace to you and peace from God our Father and the Lord Jesus Christ.

continue

ADDRESS

Romans 1:1-15

1:1-7 Greeting

Paul begins by using the conventional Greco-Roman letter opening: sender to recipients, and greetings. A bare-bones opening would be "Paul, to the church in Rome, greetings." But Paul adds details to these elements and makes other adaptations. It is important to pay attention to these additions and adaptations because he tends to foreshadow key themes through them that he will take up in the letter itself.

In identifying himself, Paul's description takes four full verses (1:1-4; compare, e.g., 1 Thess 1:1). This is no surprise given that he has yet to step foot in Rome and most in the community have not met him in person. His first self-description, "slave of Christ Jesus," can be jarring, especially in our cultural context today. In Paul's time, slavery was an accepted institution, but he is not glorifying it. What he intends to express via this imagery is that he belongs completely to Jesus and is fully committed to doing his will. Later in the letter, he will express the paradox that, in choosing to serve Christ, he experiences true freedom.

As is typical of Paul, he then identifies himself as an apostle. Though he was not one of the Twelve whom Jesus called during his earthly ministry, Paul's title signals that he has had an encounter with the risen Lord and has been "sent" (the meaning of the word "apostle") by him on a particular mission. His use of the phrase "set apart" evokes the calls of the prophets Isaiah and Jeremiah (Isa 6:7; Jer 1:5). He has been set apart for the work of "the gospel of God." Throughout the letter, Paul makes clear that *God* is the one who has acted through Jesus and the Spirit, and who continues to work through ministers like himself.

The word "gospel" means "good news," and we will see shortly how the apostle appreciates the salvific nature of the term (1:16-17). The gospel that Paul proclaims is about Jesus, about whom Paul says two important things. First, Jesus is descended from David; hence, he is the long-awaited Messiah (the Hebrew equivalent of the Greek term for "Christ," which means the "anointed one"). This is the earliest attestation in the New Testament of Jesus' physical descent from David. Second, Jesus is God's Son, shown by his being raised from the dead through the power of the Holy Spirit. The apostle's wording is a bit tricky here, but his meaning is that Jesus' resurrection confirmed who he always was: Son of God and Lord. Paul adds an important detail—namely, that what God has done through Jesus had been promised and foretold through the prophets.

Paul's identity and call, which he describes as the "grace of apostleship," are thus inextricably linked to the gospel he is called to proclaim. His mission is "to bring about the obedience of faith," especially among the Gentiles—hence a reason for writing to the Romans, among whom were Gentiles in the community of faith. Faith and obedience are two related themes that permeate the letter. These are the appropriate human response to the proclamation of the gospel. They are also key characteristics of Jesus in his relationship with the Father.

Interestingly, Paul does not identify the recipients as "church," probably because they met in several house churches. Instead, he describes them as "beloved of God." Their identity as Christians is grounded in God's love for them. In fact, God's love is a central theme of the letter, bracketing chapters 5–8. The Christian community in Rome is called to be holy, the fundamental vocation of those who have been gifted with the presence of the Holy Spirit (5:5). As the letter proceeds, Paul will offer the Roman Christians many ways in which they can grow in holiness.

The apostle then adapts and expands upon the greeting itself. The Greek word for "greeting" is *chairein*, which he changes to *charis*, a term usually translated "grace." It refers to the sheer gifted quality of the life God offers through Jesus. Indeed, Paul's letters are permeated with this word. One reason is that he himself experienced the unmerited giftedness of God's love when he was called to his ministry—while persecuting the church (see Acts 9; 1 Cor 15:9). He never forgot God's love and goodness to him, offered even as he was acting as an enemy of the gospel. Paul then adds the wish of divine "peace" (a typical Jewish greeting, which in Hebrew is *shalom*). His greeting is transformed into a prayer, as he calls forth God's gifts upon the community of faith in Rome.

"Grace to you and peace from God our Father and the Lord Jesus Christ" (1:7). This greeting, common in Paul's letters in one form or another, has become a standard **liturgical formula** in the Mass and other worship services.

Thanksgiving

[8]First, I give thanks to my God through Jesus Christ for all of you, because your faith is heralded throughout the world. [9]God is my witness, whom I serve with my spirit in proclaiming the gospel of his Son, that I remember you constantly, [10]always asking in my prayers that somehow by God's will I may at last find my way clear to come to you. [11]For I long to see you, that I may share with you some spiritual gift so that you may be strengthened, [12]that is, that you and I may be mutually encouraged by one another's faith, yours and mine. [13]I do not want you to be unaware, brothers, that I often planned to come to you, though I was prevented until now, that I might harvest some fruit among you, too, as among the rest of the Gentiles. [14]To Greeks and non-Greeks alike, to the wise and the ignorant, I am under obligation; [15]that is why I am eager to preach the gospel also to you in Rome.

continue

1:8-15 Thanksgiving

Following the opening greeting, Greco-Roman letters typically featured a thanksgiving prayer to the gods. Paul offers thanksgiving to the one God. He thanks God for the faithful response of the Roman Christians to the gospel. The apostle thereby models the good pastoral practice of affirming the gifts of those to whom one ministers. He also expresses to them his long-standing desire to visit them in person. In doing so, notice how he both encourages the community and shares his affection for them.

He wants to bolster their faith, as well as their trust in him. The language of harvesting fruit from them is an allusion to both a spiritual harvest and to the financial and logistical assistance he will ask from them for the mission to Spain.

Who was St. Paul?

St. Paul is without a doubt one of the most fascinating personalities in the New Testament. His life and letters have had an immeasurable impact on Christian theology and spirituality.

Paul was a Diaspora Jew, born in the city of Tarsus (in modern Turkey) between 1 and 10 CE. "Paul" is the Greek version of his Jewish name "Saul" (Acts 13:9). Paul was at home in both the Jewish and Gentile worlds of his time.

Little is known of Paul's early life and upbringing, although he provides numerous personal details in his letters (e.g., Phil 3:4-6). Acts says that Paul was educated in Jerusalem by the great rabbi Gamaliel (22:3), which may account for his extensive knowledge of the Jewish Scriptures. Like his mentor Gamaliel, Paul belonged to the Pharisees, a party of laymen and scribes who were often at odds with the priestly Sadducees. Both Paul and the author of Acts acknowledge that he was a zealous Jew who persecuted the early church (Acts 9:1-2; 1 Cor 15:8-10; Gal 1:13-24).

Acts goes on to describe Paul's conversion on the road to Damascus (9:1-19), something that Paul recounts in his letters only in rather vague terms as a "revelation of Jesus Christ" (Gal 1:12). This event transformed Paul from one of the church's most ardent opponents to its most articulate promoter. Although we label this moment Paul's "conversion," it is portrayed more properly as a prophetic "call" such as that of Isaiah, Jeremiah, or Ezekiel. This divine call focused primarily on Paul as "the apostle to the Gentiles" (see Acts 9:15; Rom 1:13). Most of Paul's communities were likely a mixture of both Jews and Gentiles, but Paul's primary mission was to the Gentile world, where he experienced his greatest success as an apostle and missionary.

Paul's primary legacy has been left to the church in his letters, all of which predate the canonical Gospels by decades (ca. 51–62 CE). Paul traveled extensively throughout the Mediterranean region, founding many churches and preaching the gospel (the "good news"). He also visited Christian communities that he did not found (e.g., Colossae, Rome), often expanding and further interpreting the good news of Jesus Christ.

Paul used letters, usually sent by couriers, as a primary means of ongoing contact with these communities. The New Testament contains thirteen letters attributed to Paul, but there were surely many other letters that have been lost to history. Paul never intended to write a systematic treatise about the Christian faith, but his letters are the source of many Christian ideas that have been developed within the church over the centuries.

Paul must have been an incredibly strong individual. He traveled tirelessly, endured many hardships (2 Cor 11:23-29), and was willing to challenge other leading Christian authorities when he thought it was warranted (e.g., Acts 15; Gal 2). While the New Testament does not record Paul's death by beheading, ancient tradition places his death in Rome around the same time as Peter's martyrdom, most likely under the persecution of Christians by the emperor Nero in the early 60s CE.

Paul called himself "the least of the apostles" (1 Cor 15:9), but he is widely considered to be the greatest Christian missionary of all time.

II: Humanity Lost without the Gospel

God's Power for Salvation

[16]For I am not ashamed of the gospel. It is the power of God for the salvation of everyone who believes: for Jew first, and then Greek. [17]For in it is revealed the righteousness of God from faith to faith; as it is written, "The one who is righteous by faith will live."

continue

HUMANITY LOST WITHOUT THE GOSPEL

Romans 1:16–3:20

1:16-17 God's Power for Salvation

The body or main content of the letter begins here. Using the literary device of understatement ("I am not ashamed"), Paul says, in effect, that he is proud of the gospel he proclaims. Mention of not being ashamed alludes to his recognition that the message of God working through a crucified Messiah was something that many people found difficult to comprehend (see, e.g., 1 Cor 1:18). But, as the apostle will insist, God's power and love are revealed through the cross.

Paul is clear that the message of the crucified and risen Jesus, the gospel, has the power to save. The word "power" is *dynamis,* from which we get words like "dynamic" and even "dynamite." For Paul, the gospel is a performative word. That is, it powerfully effects or brings about what it proclaims when people open their hearts to receive it. His statement concerning "Jew first, and then Greek" is a recognition of the special role that Israel plays in salvation history. Here "Greek" is synonymous with "Gentile." God's salvation is on offer to all peoples (see 1 Tim 2:4).

A key point introduced here is that the gospel reveals "the righteousness of God." This is our first encounter with this important phrase for Paul. It refers most fundamentally to God's covenant faithfulness, a fidelity that endures, even in the face of human infidelity.

A word about covenant will be helpful in this context. "Covenant" expresses God's initiative in establishing a special relationship with people (e.g., with the people of Israel following the exodus from Egypt). The Israelites agreed to become God's people, under God's special protection and care. In doing so, they received the law, which taught them the ways of God's holiness, to which they were to bear witness to the nations. The covenant had two related dimensions: a vertical one (how to relate to God) and a horizontal one (how to relate to fellow members of the community). It is crucial to appreciate that there is no such thing as a one-dimensional "God and me" spirituality in the Bible. To be in relationship with God also entails being in relationship with others. This is why Jesus answered the question about the greatest commandment by citing *two* commandments: Love God with your whole being (Deut 6:5), and love your neighbor as yourself (Lev 19:18).

The phrase "from faith to faith" has been understood in different ways. As will become clear in 3:21-22, it points to both a source of faith and the purpose or goal of God's faithfulness. The source of faith is hinted at in the Scripture quotation from the prophet Habakkuk that follows ("The one who is righteous by faith will live"; see Hab 2:4). Recall that the apostle has already indicated that the gospel concerning God's Son was foretold through the prophets (1:2). Here is the very first quotation from a prophet, a fact that suggests that it pertains to Jesus. Jesus is the "righteous one" (see, e.g., Acts 3:14) whose faithfulness to God's will has brought about the possibility of salvation. Here is the first instance of Paul reading Scripture through what we may call "christological lenses."

1:18-32 Punishment of Idolaters

Immediately following his brief description of the revelation of God's righteousness, Paul turns suddenly to discussing the revelation of the "wrath of God." The divine wrath needs to be understood carefully. The apostle begins to explain the context of universal sinfulness into which God's covenant fidelity has been revealed. Paul holds that human beings—and here he has in mind Gentiles—should be able to reason to the existence and goodness of God from the grandeur of creation. But they are guilty of two offenses. One is "impiety" or godlessness, by which Paul refers to their failure to recognize and give proper worship to God. Notice how this involves the vertical dimension of covenant relationships. It can be easy to fail to acknowledge God and, instead, to make "gods" of created things. This dynamic, idolatry—the major offense of Gentiles, in Paul's mind—still plays out today, often in more subtle ways. A good self-examination is to ask ourselves: To whom or to what do I find myself giving my attention, time, disposable resources, and energy? The answer to that question may reveal the "idols" in our own lives.

The second offense is "wickedness," by which Paul points, in one broad brushstroke, to the underlying cause of the breakdown of justice and human relationships. The list of vices in 1:29-31 is illustrative of the attitudes and behaviors that break down communities—that is, that negatively impact the horizontal dimension of covenant.

God's "wrath" refers here to God allowing people to suffer the consequences of their impiety and wickedness, indicated by the repetition of the clause "God handed them over." Divine wrath is not arbitrary or vindictive but, rather, the result of human rebellion against God and God's ways. In this way, it is an aspect of divine righteousness.

Paul then lists a number of ways in which God has allowed this rebellion to play out. One way—in homosexual relations—calls for further explanation. Romans 1:26-27 has often been cited in relation to the matter of homosexuality. There is no doubt that, as a Jew, Paul would have seen homosexual relations as unnatural and against God's plan (and as a classic example of Gentile sinfulness). But to focus on these two verses as a blanket condemnation that says everything there is to say on the topic

Punishment of Idolaters

[18]The wrath of God is indeed being revealed
from heaven against every impiety and wicked-
ness of those who suppress the truth by their wick-
edness. [19]For what can be known about God is
evident to them, because God made it evident to
them. [20]Ever since the creation of the world, his
invisible attributes of eternal power and divinity
have been able to be understood and perceived in
what he has made. As a result, they have no ex-
cuse; [21]for although they knew God they did not
accord him glory as God or give him thanks. In-
stead, they became vain in their reasoning, and
their senseless minds were darkened. [22]While
claiming to be wise, they became fools [23]and ex-
changed the glory of the immortal God for the
likeness of an image of mortal man or of birds or
of four-legged animals or of snakes.

[24]Therefore, God handed them over to impu-
rity through the lusts of their hearts for the mu-
tual degradation of their bodies. [25]They exchanged
the truth of God for a lie and revered and wor-
shiped the creature rather than the creator, who
is blessed forever. Amen. [26]Therefore, God handed
them over to degrading passions. Their females
exchanged natural relations for unnatural, [27]and
the males likewise gave up natural relations with
females and burned with lust for one another.
Males did shameful things with males and thus
received in their own persons the due penalty for
their perversity. [28]And since they did not see fit
to acknowledge God, God handed them over to
their undiscerning mind to do what is improper.
[29]They are filled with every form of wickedness,
evil, greed, and malice; full of envy, murder, ri-
valry, treachery, and spite. They are gossips [30]and
scandalmongers and they hate God. They are in-
solent, haughty, boastful, ingenious in their wick-
edness, and rebellious toward their parents.
[31]They are senseless, faithless, heartless, ruthless.
[32]Although they know the just decree of God that
all who practice such things deserve death, they
not only do them but give approval to those who
practice them.

continue

CHAPTER 2

God's Just Judgment

1Therefore, you are without excuse, every one of you who passes judgment. For by the standard by which you judge another you condemn yourself, since you, the judge, do the very same things. 2We know that the judgment of God on those who do such things is true. 3Do you suppose, then, you who judge those who engage in such things and yet do them yourself, that you will escape the judgment of God? 4Or do you hold his priceless kindness, forbearance, and patience in low esteem, unaware that the kindness of God would lead you to repentance? 5By your stubbornness and impenitent heart, you are storing up wrath for yourself for the day of wrath and revelation of the just judgment of God, 6who will repay everyone according to his works: 7eternal life to those who seek glory, honor, and immortality through perseverance in good works, 8but wrath and fury to those who selfishly disobey the truth and obey wickedness. 9Yes, affliction and distress will come upon every human being who does evil, Jew first and then Greek. 10But there will be glory, honor, and peace for everyone who does good, Jew first and then Greek. 11There is no partiality with God.

continue

puts too much burden on them. It is striking how infrequently the apostle brings up the issue (elsewhere, only in 1 Cor 6:9-10 and 1 Tim 1:9-10). He is more concerned, throughout his letters, with addressing attitudes and behaviors that break down relationships and communities, such as those listed in 1:29-31. The topic of the present passage is not homosexuality but the failure to recognize and honor God. This failure has consequences for those who are created in God's image but do not honor that image in one another.

2:1-11 God's Just Judgment

Paul now takes up the issue of judgment by conversing with an imaginary interlocutor who passes judgment on others. This paragraph serves two functions. First, the apostle warns against people passing judgment on one another. This is God's prerogative, not ours, for only God knows what is in human hearts (2:16). Not only that, but human judgment is often flawed, as we tend to condemn in others what we do not like about ourselves. We can easily be guilty of hypocrisy, or doing the same things we condemn in others.

Paul uses the literary device of **diatribe** (see Introduction) throughout Romans 2. Other examples of diatribe in Romans include 3:27-31 and 7:1-25.

Second, because God's character is righteous, Paul insists that God judges with impartiality on the basis of people's works. But notice that God's sense of justice is also tempered by "kindness, forbearance, and patience." These merciful divine attributes (so important for us to remember whenever we turn to God in prayer) are not to be taken for granted, however. They should motivate us to repent of our sinful ways, including our proclivity to judge others.

Paul then offers a simple yet beautiful description of a way of living that leads to God's bestowal of eternal life. We are to seek God's glory, by which he means those things that give honor to God (and not to ourselves). And we are to persevere in "do[ing] good," which is the basis of divine judgment. Some readers might be surprised to read Paul's emphasis on the importance of good works. Since the time of Martin Luther, much stress has been put on the apostle's insistence on faith over works. We will have occasion to explain Paul's meaning as we work our way through the letter, but let us keep in mind his accent here on the necessity of good works.

2:12-16 Judgment by the Interior Law

To illustrate God's fairness and impartiality, Paul anticipates a possible objection. While the Jews have been given the Mosaic law, what about the Gentiles? Here we encounter the first reference to the Jewish law, a theme to which we will have many occasions to return. Paul insists that Gentiles will not be judged on its basis, for that would not be fair. They will be judged on another basis, the basis of the "law" of conscience, that God-given inner forum of moral discernment bestowed on all people. This gift of conscience provides them with the wherewithal to know and obey God and God's ways. It is in following the law of conscience that Gentiles can be considered obedient or disobedient inwardly to God's law. Here "law" refers to that which constitutes moral goodness, not to specific practices like Sabbath observance.

Paul is one of the first people in history (if not *the* first) to insist on the primacy of conscience. Indeed, elsewhere he argues that a person's conscience should determine moral decision-making, and that one should never act, or be forced to act, against one's conscience (see, e.g., 1 Cor 10:23-29).

2:17-29 Judgment by the Mosaic Law

Up to this point, Paul's focus has been on the Gentiles and their sinful ways. One can imagine Jewish members of the house churches in Rome nodding their heads in agreement at the apostle's assessment of Gentiles that began in 1:18. But now Paul turns the tables. It is not only the Gentiles who have failed. So too have the Jews, who were gifted with the Mosaic law and were proud of this gift—including, for males, the command to bear the mark of circumcision. But it is not enough to possess the law; it must be internalized in obedience.

Paul's critique includes what he perceives to be the Jews' failure to be a guide and a light for the Gentiles. When entering into covenant with Israel, God commanded, "Be holy, for I, the Lord your God, am holy" (Lev 19:2). One of Israel's fundamental responsibilities, as God's covenant people, was to show forth to the nations the holiness and goodness of God. The accusation of robbing temples, one example of failure, probably refers to the practice of taking things of value from pagan shrines

Judgment by the Interior Law

12All who sin outside the law will also perish without reference to it, and all who sin under the law will be judged in accordance with it. 13For it is not those who hear the law who are just in the sight of God; rather, those who observe the law will be justified. 14For when the Gentiles who do not have the law by nature observe the prescriptions of the law, they are a law for themselves even though they do not have the law. 15They show that the demands of the law are written in their hearts, while their conscience also bears witness and their conflicting thoughts accuse or even defend them 16on the day when, according to my gospel, God will judge people's hidden works through Christ Jesus.

Judgment by the Mosaic Law

17Now if you call yourself a Jew and rely on the law and boast of God 18and know his will and are able to discern what is important since you are instructed from the law, 19and if you are confident that you are a guide for the blind and a light for those in darkness, 20that you are a trainer of the foolish and teacher of the simple, because in the law you have the formulation of knowledge and truth— 21then you who teach another, are you failing to teach yourself? You who preach against stealing, do you steal? 22You who forbid adultery, do you commit adultery? You who detest idols, do you rob temples? 23You who boast of the law, do you dishonor God by breaking the law? 24For, as it is written, "Because of you the name of God is reviled among the Gentiles."

25Circumcision, to be sure, has value if you observe the law; but if you break the law, your circumcision has become uncircumcision. 26Again, if an uncircumcised man keeps the precepts of the law, will he not be considered circumcised? 27Indeed, those who are physically uncircumcised but carry out the law will pass judgment on you, with your written law and circumcision, who break the law. 28One is not a Jew outwardly. True circumcision is not outward, in

continue

the flesh. [29]Rather, one is a Jew inwardly, and circumcision is of the heart, in the spirit, not the letter; his praise is not from human beings but from God.

CHAPTER 3

Answers to Objections

[1]What advantage is there then in being a Jew? Or what is the value of circumcision? [2]Much, in every respect. [For] in the first place, they were entrusted with the utterances of God. [3]What if some were unfaithful? Will their infidelity nullify the fidelity of God? [4]Of course not! God must be true, though every human being is a liar, as it is written:

"That you may be justified in your words,
and conquer when you are judged."

[5]But if our wickedness provides proof of God's righteousness, what can we say? Is God unjust, humanly speaking, to inflict his wrath? [6]Of course not! For how else is God to judge the world? [7]But if God's truth redounds to his glory through my falsehood, why am I still being condemned as a sinner? [8]And why not say—as we are accused and as some claim we say—that we should do evil that good may come of it? Their penalty is what they deserve.

continue

and temples under the pretext that the so-called "gods" honored in them did not really exist. It is unclear how widespread this practice was.

Related to Israel's call to collective holiness, it is good for Catholics to reflect on what *Lumen Gentium*, the Second Vatican Council's Dogmatic Constitution on the Church, says about the church's fundamental call. The church is to be "the universal sacrament of salvation," the incarnation of Christ's love in and for the world (LG 48). With the gift of being church comes the responsibility of the vocation to holiness. In reading this passage from Romans, we do well to reflect on our own successes and failures in living out this call.

Unlike medical circumcision, which is a religiously neutral procedure that is chosen by many families for their sons, **circumcision** as referenced in Scripture is a religious ceremony practiced by the Jewish people that marks a child as a member of God's covenant people. Religious circumcision is an external sign that symbolizes an internal reality: a deep and lifelong relationship with God.

3:1-8 Answers to Objections

Following the critique above, Paul raises the question: Then what advantage is there to being a Jew? As a Jew himself (one who now believes Jesus is Messiah and who has become a missionary and apostle of this Messiah), Paul insists on the blessings the Jews have received. One of these blessings is the "utterances of God," a reference to the divinely revealed law and, more broadly, to all of Scripture. He goes on to assert that just because some Jews have been unfaithful to the law, that does not mean that God's faithfulness has failed. Such is a mark of God's righteousness. God is ever faithful. But as one who is righteous, God's wrath—or God's allowing people to suffer the consequences of their disobedience to God—is also shown to the Jews. Paradoxically, then, Israel's infidelities are an occasion for God to prove God's character as righteous and fair.

This leads to a dangerous question: If human infidelity leads to the demonstration of God's fidelity, then why are they subject to divine wrath? And why not sin so that God can show forth divine righteousness? This was apparently one of the false rumors against Paul's teaching, as we will see. The apostle shrugs off these questions as preposterous.

3:9-20 Universal Bondage to Sin

Paul now brings to a conclusion his gloomy assessment of the human condition before the coming of Christ. After conceding that Jews are not "entirely" better off, despite the gift of the law, he strikingly describes the human condition without Christ as being "under the domination of sin." This assessment tells us a good deal about Paul's understanding of the need for salvation and what this salvation involves. First, Paul personifies the notion of sin (thus my capitalization of "Sin" going forward). Readers should appreciate that, for Paul, Sin does not refer to individual transgressions like lying and stealing. As we will see in Romans 5, Sin—along with Death, which is also personified—is a malevolent cosmic force that was unleashed at the disobedience of Adam. Sin and Death are the two great enemies of humankind. Second, Sin exercises its tyranny by enslavement, by entrapping people into sinful habits and patterns from which they cannot extricate themselves.

This metaphor of enslavement (think of the enslavement of the Hebrews in Egypt) is background for one of the ways Paul talks about how we have been saved through Christ. The language and imagery of "redemption" refers, in its most basic sense, to the ransoming or buying back of a family member who has been captured (e.g., as a prisoner of war). The apostle does not discriminate between Jews and Gentiles. Since all have been complicit in disobedience, all are in need of redemption. The "ransom" or "price" paid is the life of Jesus Christ (see Mark 10:45; 1 Cor 6:20).

Universal Bondage to Sin

9Well, then, are we better off? Not entirely, for we have already brought the charge against Jews and Greeks alike that they are all under the domination of sin, 10as it is written:

"There is no one just, not one,
11there is no one who understands,
there is no one who seeks God.
12All have gone astray; all alike are worthless;
there is not one who does good,
[there is not] even one.
13Their throats are open graves;
they deceive with their tongues;
the venom of asps is on their lips;
14their mouths are full of bitter cursing.
15Their feet are quick to shed blood;
16ruin and misery are in their ways,
17and the way of peace they know not.
18There is no fear of God before their eyes."

19Now we know that what the law says is addressed to those under the law, so that every mouth may be silenced and the whole world stand accountable to God, 20since no human being will be justified in his sight by observing the law; for through the law comes consciousness of sin.

Paul then cites a series of passages from Scripture (Ecclesiastes, Isaiah, and a good number from Psalms) that bear witness to the universality of human sinfulness. Paul is clearly serious about the ongoing message and relevance of the sacred texts. Notice the number of body parts mentioned (e.g., throats, lips, eyes). The enslaving power of Sin is all-pervasive. The phrase "There is no one" is like a refrain, giving poignant emphasis to the universality of sin among Gentiles and Jews. Indeed, the rhetorical effect of this widely cast scriptural witness is that every mouth is silenced before God. The imagery here is that of the courtroom: There is no one who can offer a defense before the righteous God.

Paul then makes the first of a number of asides about the law that will appear in this letter. Here Paul says that no one will be "justified" before God through observance of the law. At this point, he says that the law functions to make people aware of their sinfulness.

A word about the verb "justify" is in order. It comes from the same root as the noun that is translated "righteousness." For Paul, "justify" has a legal sense: It means to be declared "not guilty" by God. It also entails being named as part of God's covenant people. This is very important for the Gentiles, and we will see that part of the challenge of the early church was determining how Gentiles were to be included in the covenant people. In addition, as Paul will point out in his teaching on the Holy Spirit, the verb rendered "justify" also entails a transformative element: People are made righteous through the gift of the Spirit.

We are now on the brink of Paul's full statement about the revelation of God's righteousness, starting in 3:21. What he has done up to this point has been to set the stage for the saving action of the ever-faithful God. The gloomy darkness of the apostle's description of human disobedience and wickedness will serve to make the light of salvation all the more brilliant.

EXPLORING LESSON ONE

1. Which of the themes mentioned in the Introduction are you most looking forward to learning about in Paul's Letter to the Romans and why?

2. Why does Paul write this letter to the community in Rome? What does Paul provide for the Roman Christians in his letter, and what does he hope to gain from them?

3. How would you describe "the righteousness of God" as understood by Paul, a key theme of the Letter to the Romans?

4. Why does Paul consider himself to be an apostle (1:1)?

5. Paul greets the Romans with the word "grace" (1:7). What is grace, and how was Paul personally transformed by God's grace?

6. a) What are the two dimensions of a covenant relationship (1:16-17; Mark 12:28-34)? What are some ways you live the horizontal dimension of your covenant relationship with God?

   b) How does Paul's assessment of human sin (1:18-32) address both the vertical and horizontal aspects of the covenant?

7. What wisdom do you find in Paul's words about human and divine judgment in 2:1-11?

8. Paul insists that although Gentiles are not held to the standards of the Jewish law, they are still bound to the law of conscience, which is "written in their hearts" (2:15). Reflect on your own conscience and how it has guided you throughout your life. When have you listened to it? When have you neglected it? What were the results?

9. Just as Israel was given the great responsibility of being a light to the Gentiles (Isa 42:6), so we as believers are to be signs of God's love in the world (2:17-29). What are some ways you believe the church has been successful in being this sign? What are some ways we have fallen short, and how can we do better?

10. What is Paul's understanding of sin (or Sin, as it is personified in the letter) and its power over human beings (3:9-20)?

CLOSING PRAYER

Prayer

Ever since the creation of the world, [God's] invisible attributes of eternal power and divinity have been able to be understood and perceived in what he has made. (Rom 1:20)

Loving God, Creator of all things, open our eyes to the goodness and beauty of creation. Help us to recognize in creation the gifts of your love, including every person, created in your image and likeness. May we always give you thanks and praise, and honor you by being in right relationship with others. We pray today especially for . . .

LESSON TWO

Romans 3:21–5:21

Begin your personal study and group discussion with a simple and sincere prayer such as:

Prayer

Loving God, send your Spirit upon us as we study the writings of your apostle Paul. Open our ears, our minds, and especially our hearts. Deepen your love within us, and transform us to embody and proclaim the good news you have revealed in your son Jesus Christ.

Read the Bible text of Romans 3:21–5:21, found in the outside columns of pages 32–41, highlighting what stands out to you.

Read the accompanying commentary to add to your understanding.

Respond to the questions on pages 42–44, Exploring Lesson Two.

The Closing Prayer on page 45 is for your personal use and may be used at the end of group discussion.

III. Justification through Faith in Christ

Justification Apart from the Law

[21]But now the righteousness of God has been
manifested apart from the law, though testified
to by the law and the prophets, [22]the righteousness
of God through faith in Jesus Christ for all who
believe. For there is no distinction; [23]all have
sinned and are deprived of the glory of God.
[24]They are justified freely by his grace through the
redemption in Christ Jesus, [25]whom God set forth
as an expiation, through faith, by his blood, to
prove his righteousness because of the forgiveness
of sins previously committed, [26]through the for-
bearance of God—to prove his righteousness in
the present time, that he might be righteous and
justify the one who has faith in Jesus.
[27]What occasion is there then for boasting? It
is ruled out. On what principle, that of works?
No, rather on the principle of faith. [28]For we con-
sider that a person is justified by faith apart from
works of the law. [29]Does God belong to Jews
alone? Does he not belong to Gentiles, too? Yes,
also to Gentiles, [30]for God is one and will justify
the circumcised on the basis of faith and the un-
circumcised through faith. [31]Are we then annul-
ling the law by this faith? Of course not! On the
contrary, we are supporting the law.

continue

JUSTIFICATION THROUGH FAITH IN CHRIST

Romans 3:21–5:21

3:21-31 Justification Apart from the Law

With the small but momentous word "now," Paul proclaims what the righteous God has done in the face of universal human disobedience. In 3:21-22 he unpacks and expands on what he wrote earlier in 1:17 about the revelation of God's righteousness and its relationship to the notion of faith. Given the importance of this sentence and paragraph for the apostle's presentation of the gospel, we will work our way through them with great care.

When Paul writes that God's righteousness "has been manifested," he uses a verb tense (the perfect tense in Greek) that signifies something that happened in the past that has ongoing ramifications in the present. That God's righteousness has been manifested "apart from the law" signifies that the way by which God brings about right relationship with people is not through their adherence to the dictates of the Jewish law (e.g., Sabbath observance; dietary regulations/kosher foods; and, for men, circumcision). Nevertheless, the revelation of God's righteousness is "testified to by the law and the prophets"—that is, by the testimony of Scripture. We have seen that Paul has already attested that the prophets foretold what God would do through Jesus. Now he adds that the first five books of the Bible (the Pentateuch, or Torah, which is translated into "law" in Greek) also attest to God's saving action. Notice how he uses the same term ("law") to refer both to the commandments contained in those books and to the five books themselves. Moreover, Paul also at times uses "law" to refer to Scripture as a whole (at least, what we would call the Old Testament). This can, at times, cause confusion, and we will have to pay careful attention to these distinctions as we go along.

How, then, has God's righteousness been manifested? Here we arrive at a disputed point among Pauline scholars. The New American Bible, Revised Edition (NABRE; the translation we are using) renders the Greek as "through faith in Jesus Christ for all who believe." While that seems straightforward enough, there is another possibility. "Faith in Christ" renders a two-word phrase in Greek: *pistis Christou*. Both *pistis* ("faith") and *Christou* ("Christ") are nouns, and the interpretive challenge is to determine the relationship between them. To offer an example from English, the phrase "love of God" can refer to God's love for us or our love for God. We rely on context to know which is meant. Similarly, in addition to meaning "faith *in* Christ," *pistis Christou* can also mean "faith *of* Christ," as in "Christ's faith" or "Christ's faithfulness." So, which is it here?

Some scholars, myself included, argue that, given how Paul has relentlessly set forth the sinfulness of all humanity, it would be strange if God's righteousness and justice were revealed in the *human* act of faith and believing. Recall also that, at the beginning of the letter, Paul refers to the good news about *what God has done* in and through Jesus (1:1-7). Moreover, in the sentences that follow here, we will see several references to Jesus' self-offering on the cross. Thus, I propose that we understand Paul as saying that God's righteousness has been revealed through the *faithfulness of Jesus* the Messiah. This interpretation helps explain the use of the perfect tense verb—something happened (Christ's death) that has ongoing implications (even to now!). It also removes a potential redundancy created by the sentence's closing phrase, "for all who believe." Indeed, this latter phrase is better understood as expressing the purpose or goal of God's action in Christ: "to bring about faith [or faithfulness]" (my translation)—that is, to bring about the appropriate human response to the gospel.

Paul proceeds to argue that, because all have sinned, there is "no distinction" among peoples in terms of their need for salvation. All have fallen short and have tarnished the image of God in which they were created. The one God, who is just and fair, reaches out to all peoples in the same way: namely, through

CHAPTER 4

Abraham Justified by Faith

1 What then can we say that Abraham found, our ancestor according to the flesh? 2 Indeed, if Abraham was justified on the basis of his works, he has reason to boast; but this was not so in the sight of God. 3 For what does the scripture say? "Abraham believed God, and it was credited to him as righteousness." 4 A worker's wage is credited not as a gift, but as something due. 5 But when one does not work, yet believes in the one who justifies the ungodly, his faith is credited as righteousness. 6 So also David declares the blessedness of the person to whom God credits righteousness apart from works:

7 "Blessed are they whose iniquities are
forgiven
and whose sins are covered.
8 Blessed is the man whose sin the Lord does
not record."

continue

Christ and his redemptive death, one that frees us from sinful ways. His death is also "expiation"—that is, a sacrifice for sin. Note how the apostle refers to this sacrificial death as "through faith, by his blood"; that is, through Jesus' faithfulness-unto-death, God offers right relationship (with God and others). Indeed, while God was forbearing and patient all along, God has now dealt with the problem of human disobedience and sin. Divine justice is tempered by mercy as God offers to "justify"—to bring to right relationship—those who "share in the faithfulness of Jesus" (my translation; 3:26). This translation (which differs from the NABRE translation: "the one who has faith in Jesus") is in line with what we just discussed. It points to how, through the gospel, God wants to form a people who, like Jesus, are committed fully to the divine will and who live for the sake of others.

The offer of salvation through Christ is thus pure gift: We "are justified freely by [God's] grace." This is not something *we* can accomplish; thus there is no room for human boasting. Both Jews and Gentiles are saved by faith—first and foremost, by the faithfulness of Jesus. When Paul contrasts "faith" and "works" here (3:27-28), he is contrasting Jesus' faithfulness with "works of the [Jewish] law," or those things such as Sabbath observance, food laws, and circumcision that are unique to Jews. As we will see, the apostle insists that God desires to form a single family, consisting of Jews and Gentiles, whose distinguishing characteristic is faithfulness to God after the manner of Jesus. In doing so, Paul denies that he annuls the law (in terms of obeying its demands). Rather, he upholds the law. Here, "law" refers more broadly to the story of Scripture starting with Genesis, as the story of Abraham that follows will show.

4:1-8 Abraham Justified by Faith (First Emphasis)

The figure of Abraham looms large for Jews, given his role as the one who first entered into a covenant relationship with God and who was promised a numerous people and bounteous land. Moreover, it was Abraham who first received circumcision at God's command, a physical and outward sign of belonging to God.

In light of God's action through Jesus' faithfulness-unto-death, Paul now retells the story of Abraham with three particular emphases. First, in 4:1-8, he argues that Scripture itself, even from the very start (the Book of Genesis), points to the primacy of faith as marking Abraham's relationship with God. The apostle repeatedly cites Genesis 15:6—"Abraham believed God, and it was credited to him as righteousness"—in order to link the notion of trusting faith with the bestowal of God's righteous status on Abraham (that is, with Abraham's belonging to God). In addition, Paul cites Psalm 32:1-2 to indicate something that God no longer accounted (or reckoned) to Abraham: his sins, which were forgiven. This is part of receiving the status of being righteous from God. It is important to appreciate that, when God called Abraham, Abraham was among the "ungodly," those worshiping other gods. But his response to God was very different from that of the ungodly Paul described in 1:18-32.

So what did Abraham find or learn (4:1)? He found that, in placing his unwavering and faithful trust in God's extraordinary promises to bestow on him offspring beyond counting and a bounteous land, he was credited with the bestowal of the status of righteous standing before God and made the father of a people (in the first place, the Jews). Moreover, his sins were, in effect, *dis*credited, as he was forgiven, an essential aspect of this new standing.

Justification is God's free act of declaring people righteous, by which they receive the gift of salvation. Martin Luther viewed this concept as Paul's primary teaching and believed that Catholics overemphasized "earning" salvation by performing righteous deeds. In 1999, Lutherans and Catholics reached a landmark agreement on the teaching of justification by faith. The agreement clarified each denomination's position and demonstrated a common approach to justification as God's free gift of salvation that is achieved, once and for all, in Jesus Christ (*Joint Declaration on the Doctrine of Justification*). In 2006, the World Methodist Council also signed on to this agreement.

4:9-17 Abraham Justified by Faith (Second Emphasis)

Paul now provides his second new emphasis in his retelling of the story of Abraham. The tradition of Abraham as the father of the Jews goes back to the promise of offspring referred to above. But now Paul makes an additional claim: Abraham is also the father of Gentiles who have come to believe in what God has done through Jesus; that is, he is the father in faith of the Jew and Gentile family, the church, that God is forming. Moreover, the apostle claims a different significance to Abraham's being circumcised. In order to appreciate his presentation, it is necessary to review the order of events as they are recounted in the Book of Genesis.

Genesis 15 tells the story of God's extravagant promises to Abraham, Abraham's trusting belief in those promises, and God's crediting this to Abraham as righteousness. All these events occurred *before* Abraham was commanded to be circumcised (which does not take place until Gen 17). What is implicit here is the priority of a faithful, trusting response to God and God's promises—not circumcision.

Paul also reinterprets what Abraham's circumcision signified. According to Genesis 17, Abraham was circumcised at God's command. Circumcision was to be the mark of Abraham and his descendants that showed forth their belonging to God. It foreshadowed Abraham's and the people's obedience to God's commands as they would be set forth in the Jewish law. In effect, circumcision was a "[work] of the law" (see 3:28).

9Does this blessedness apply only to the circumcised, or to the uncircumcised as well? Now we assert that "faith was credited to Abraham as righteousness." 10Under what circumstances was it credited? Was he circumcised or not? He was not circumcised, but uncircumcised. 11And he received the sign of circumcision as a seal on the righteousness received through faith while he was uncircumcised. Thus, he was to be the father of all the uncircumcised who believe, so that to them [also] righteousness might be credited, 12as well as the father of the circumcised who not only are circumcised but also follow the path of faith that our father Abraham walked while still uncircumcised.

Inheritance Through Faith

13It was not through the law that the promise was made to Abraham and his descendants that he would inherit the world, but through the righteousness that comes from faith. 14For if those who adhere to the law are the heirs, faith is null and the promise is void. 15For the law produces

continue

Abraham believed God, and it was credited to him as righteousness (Rom 4:3; Gen 15:6). Woodcut after a drawing by Julius Schnorr von Carolsfeld.

wrath; but where there is no law, neither is there violation. [16]For this reason, it depends on faith, so that it may be a gift, and the promise may be guaranteed to all his descendants, not to those who only adhere to the law but to those who follow the faith of Abraham, who is the father of all of us, [17]as it is written, "I have made you father of many nations." He is our father in the sight of God, in whom he believed, who gives life to the dead and calls into being what does not exist.

[18]He believed, hoping against hope, that he would become "the father of many nations," according to what was said, "Thus shall your descendants be." [19]He did not weaken in faith when he considered his own body as [already] dead (for he was almost a hundred years old) and the dead womb of Sarah. [20]He did not doubt God's promise in unbelief; rather, he was empowered by faith and gave glory to God [21]and was fully convinced that what he had promised he was also able to do. [22]That is why "it was credited to him as righteousness." [23]But it was not for him alone that it was written that "it was credited to him"; [24]it was also for us, to whom it will be credited, who believe in the one who raised Jesus our Lord from the dead, [25]who was handed over for our transgressions and was raised for our justification.

continue

But prior to this work of the law was Abraham's trusting belief in God's promises when he was uncircumcised, and Paul now names circumcision as "a seal on the righteousness received through faith." That is, he recasts circumcision as affirming the priority of faith as the distinguishing mark of God's people. Therefore, Paul claims that Abraham is the father in faith of circumcised Jews, who have responded first to God with faithful trust in imitation of Abraham, as well as of Gentiles, who respond with faith in the gospel proclamation. Thus he is "the father of all of us" and "father of many nations" (see also Gen 17:5).

Notice how Paul is prioritizing faith over law observance. He comments that the law brings wrath, because of violations against it. To be sure, we will see that Paul values the law, so we have to be careful not to draw too quick a conclusion about his valuation of God's law. The point to appreciate here is the primacy of faith for Jews and Gentiles, starting with God's covenant faithfulness in forming a Jew and Gentile family in Christ whose distinguishing characteristic is faith.

Important note: Readers will notice, especially in my exposition of the chapters that follow, that I frequently refer to the Jew and Gentile family of faith founded on the faithfulness of Abraham. This was Paul's vision of and hope for what God's action through Christ was bringing about. We need to appreciate this to understand what the apostle has set forth in Romans. As we know from history, however, Judaism and Christianity have developed into separate religions. This does not mean that God's word has failed in this connection (see 9:6); indeed, Paul insists that God remains faithful to Israel. Paul's teachings, especially in the final chapters, will offer much food for thought on how we can live as a church of diverse membership, and how Christians can relate fruitfully with our Jewish brothers and sisters.

4:18-25 Abraham Justified by Faith (Third Emphasis)

In these verses, Paul offers his third new emphasis in his retelling of the story of Abraham, as he gives a dramatic description of what Abraham's faith entailed. As we will see, the apostle's description sets the stage for what a faithful response to the gospel involves.

God's promise to Abraham—that he would be the father of a vast people—began with the divine pledge that he would father a child (Isaac). But Abraham was almost a hundred years old, and his wife Sarah was barren. Despite these seemingly impossible circumstances, Abraham was steadfast, not wavering in his trust in God. Implicit in Paul's description is that the life of faith is not a one-off response but one that entails steadfastness and perseverance. Abraham kept doing what God wanted him to do (e.g., sojourn into Egypt, in the opposite direction of the land promised to him). Abraham's faith is also described as giving glory to God—and not to oneself or to any other creature (contrast with 1:18-32). Indeed, the real key to understanding Paul's emphasis is that, though Abraham was beyond the years of fertility and Sarah's womb was "dead," God could still fulfill the divine promises because God is the Creator, the Giver of Life, who is even able to raise the dead to life. Here we can appreciate what Paul is doing vis-à-vis the gospel: The appropriate response to the gospel proclamation is trusting faith in "the one who raised Jesus our Lord from the dead." Those who do so, and who live their entire lives based on this belief, are the faithful ones to whom God credits righteousness as God did to Abraham.

Paul concludes this section with a brief Creed-like statement. In discussing Jesus' faithfulness above, we have highlighted his saving death. Here, the apostle makes clear that the saving event includes Jesus' resurrection. Through his death and resurrection, we receive forgiveness of sins ("transgressions") and are brought into right relationship with God and others ("justification").

To summarize what Paul has done in his retelling of the story of Abraham:

1. Scripture itself, from the very outset, emphasizes the primacy of a faithful response to God and God's lavish promises (hence, Paul claims that he upholds the law, understood as referring to Scripture as a whole).
2. Abraham's faith is the model not only for Jewish believers but also for Gentiles who respond with faith to the gospel proclamation. Thus Abraham is the father in faith of those who share his faith: the new family God is forming through the church.
3. This faith involves perseverance in trusting God's power, in all circumstances, to bring the dead to life, a belief manifested most dramatically in Jesus' resurrection from the dead.

CHAPTER 5

Faith, Hope, and Love

[1]Therefore, since we have been justified by
faith, we have peace with God through our Lord
Jesus Christ, [2]through whom we have gained ac-
cess [by faith] to this grace in which we stand, and
we boast in hope of the glory of God. [3]Not only
that, but we even boast of our afflictions, knowing
that affliction produces endurance, [4]and endur-
ance, proven character, and proven character,
hope, [5]and hope does not disappoint, because the
love of God has been poured out into our hearts
through the holy Spirit that has been given to us.
[6]For Christ, while we were still helpless, yet died
at the appointed time for the ungodly. [7]Indeed,
only with difficulty does one die for a just person,
though perhaps for a good person one might even
find courage to die. [8]But God proves his love for
us in that while we were still sinners Christ died
for us. [9]How much more then, since we are now
justified by his blood, will we be saved through
him from the wrath. [10]Indeed, if, while we were
enemies, we were reconciled to God through the
death of his Son, how much more, once recon-
ciled, will we be saved by his life. [11]Not only that,
but we also boast of God through our Lord Jesus
Christ, through whom we have now received rec-
onciliation.

continue

5:1-11 Faith, Hope, and Love

Paul's representation of the gospel now returns to what God has done for us through the death and resurrection of Jesus. The clause "since we have been justified by faith" refers first and foremost to Jesus' faithfulness. As discussed above, it is through Jesus' fidelity to God in offering his life that we have been brought into right relationship with God and others. Paul's wording, moreover, can be taken to include our faithful response to the gospel proclamation. He names two gifts that follow from this acceptance. First, we have "peace" with God through Jesus; second, we have "access" to God. "Peace" sets up the treatment of reconciliation that follows shortly. Similarly, "access" foreshadows what the apostle will say more immediately about the Spirit.

But before doing so, Paul offers a brief description of the growth and maturation of faith, the maturation that the story of Abraham presumed. Paul expresses this with a chain-like formulation, where the end of one clause becomes the beginning of the next. Paul begins with "afflictions." Here he is talking about the challenges, even the sufferings, that human life entails (e.g., the pain of infertility, the challenges of old age) and those that come with committing to God's ways. Faithful trust in God's promises leads not to running away from afflictions but to patiently enduring them. As noted above, the response of faith in God's promises is more than a one-off matter. It involves commitment and growth. These lead to "proven character." Thus, faith as Paul understands it produces a certain type of character, one marked by integrity. And all this leads to hope. Christian faith is always linked with hope because it is resurrection faith. Jesus' resurrection, as we will see in Romans 6 and 8, has already borne fruit in the lives of the faithful. Here Paul mentions, as one fruit of Jesus' resurrection for our lives, the gift of the Holy Spirit. How he describes this gift merits further consideration.

Notice that this gift is the means through which (or through *whom*) God's love has been bestowed upon us. Trinitarian theology developed long after Paul, but his writings were essential for its development. The Spirit is the bond of love between the Father and Son. Love by its very nature is outward focused and life-giving. Divine love has been revealed through creation and redemption. As we will see, it is revealed most definitively through Jesus and his life and death. Thus, this gift of the Spirit manifests that God's righteousness is intimately connected with divine love. This love has now been poured—an allusion to the waters of baptism—into human hearts. What a gift!

The Spirit is God-*within*-us. This gift of the Spirit is the basis of Paul's calling the believers in Rome "the beloved of God" in the opening greeting in 1:7. Romans 8 will set forth several benefits of this gift. For now, it is worth pondering the mystery that God loves us so much that God deigns to dwell in us through the Holy Spirit. This mystery can increase our appreciation of confirmation and all the sacraments, through which this gift of divine love is deepened and nourished.

In 5:6-11 Paul gives a rich description of how Jesus' faithfulness-unto-death reveals the extent of God's love for us. He first comments on how much love and courage it takes to die for another person; maybe for a truly good, just person, one might muster the courage and strength to do so. Such love, however, is rare. The apostle, in his proclamation of the "gospel of God" (1:1), offers as "proof" (3:5) of God's love for us that it was when we were most in need of God's love—most "helpless" and undeserving as "sinners"—that Jesus died for us.

It will help to unpack Paul's logic a bit here. In the first place, the sending of God's only Son shows that God holds nothing back in revealing God's love for us (see Rom 8:32; John 3:16). And in revealing God's love in his life and ministry, Jesus himself held nothing back, not even his lifeblood, in order to show the extent of divine love for us. What more "proof" do we want? (See John 15:13.) In offering his life in fidelity to God, Jesus has accomplished "justification," our being brought back to right relationship with God and others. But that is not all. Having done this, he will certainly bring us to the fullness of salvation.

Paul then makes the same point by using different imagery. Christ died for humanity "while we were enemies." To rebel against God is, as a creature, to declare one's independence from God and to seek life in fruitless ways. This is what leads to being enslaved by Sin. Only God, through Jesus' faithful death, could do something about this dire situation. Here is where the notion of "reconciliation" comes in. Reconciliation presumes a context of enmity (hence the phrase "while we were enemies"). Typically, the need for reconciliation between two parties is caused by the fault and failings on both sides, but that was not the case here. Humanity rebelled against God. But God showed magnanimity in taking the initiative to be reconciled to sinful humankind through Christ's death. Indeed, only God, the wronged or offended party, could do so. This serves as another proof of God's love. Once reconciled, we can be confident in God's desire for and commitment to our salvation. This confidence is at the heart of the gift of "peace with God." This peace is a fruit of the indwelling Spirit (see Gal 5:22), a gift that only God, in Christ, can bestow (see John 14:27).

The topic of reconciliation is important for Paul, especially in 2 Corinthians and Ephesians. In 2 Corinthians, he mentions the "message of reconciliation" and "ministry of reconciliation" that have been given to the church (2 Cor 5:18-19). We will see how that ministry can play out in intrachurch affairs later in this letter.

Humanity's Sin Through Adam

12 Therefore, just as through one person sin
entered the world, and through sin, death, and
thus death came to all, inasmuch as all sinned—
13 for up to the time of the law, sin was in the
world, though sin is not accounted when there is
no law. 14 But death reigned from Adam to Moses,
even over those who did not sin after the pattern
of the trespass of Adam, who is the type of the
one who was to come.

continue

5:12-14 Humanity's Sin Through Adam

In these verses, Paul returns to the dire situation that called forth the revelation of God's righteousness through Christ. Here he alludes to Genesis 2–3, the story of the disobedience and sin of Adam and Eve. Paul's focus on Adam (rather than both Adam and Eve) serves to present Adam as a foil for Jesus, whom Paul will present as the new Adam through whose obedience to God a new creation has come about. While the apostle likely regarded Adam as a historical figure, he also treated him as a representative figure of disobedient humankind. Romans 5:12 heavily influenced later theology, including the church's teaching on original sin. Here Paul continues to personify Sin. At Adam's disobedience to the one divine command given to him—to not eat from the tree of knowledge of good and evil (Gen 2:17)—the cosmic power of Sin was unleashed upon the world. And in the wake of Sin came Death, also personified. These are the two enslaving powers that are the great enemies of God and of what God wants for people and creation.

There is considerable debate about what Paul says at the end of 5:12 concerning the precise relationship between Adam's sin and our sinfulness. The best way to appreciate what the apostle means is that he makes two points: (1) The primordial sin unleashed the destructive powers of Sin and Death, and (2) all human beings repeat or extend Adam's disobedience in some way.

Paul then takes up an objection that is grounded on the premise that sin is not accounted where there is no law. What about the time between Adam and Moses—a lengthy amount of time before the law was given? Was Sin ruling then? The fact that people died in that period suggests that yes, it was. So too

Adam's trespass/sin	Jesus' gracious gift/righteous act
Many died	Grace abounds for many
Judgment/condemnation	Justification/acquittal
Death reigned	Recipients of life/righteousness will reign

Grace and Life Through Christ

15But the gift is not like the transgression. For
if by that one person's transgression the many
died, how much more did the grace of God and
the gift of the one person Jesus Christ overflow
for the many. 16And the gift is not like the result
of the one person's sinning. For after one sin there
was the judgment that brought condemnation;
but the gift, after many transgressions, brought
acquittal. 17For if, by the transgression of one per-
son, death came to reign through that one, how
much more will those who receive the abundance
of grace and of the gift of justification come to
reign in life through the one person Jesus Christ.
18In conclusion, just as through one transgression
condemnation came upon all, so through one
righteous act acquittal and life came to all. 19For
just as through the disobedience of one person
the many were made sinners, so through the obe-
dience of one the many will be made righteous.
20The law entered in so that transgression might
increase but, where sin increased, grace over-
flowed all the more, 21so that, as sin reigned in
death, grace also might reign through justification
for eternal life through Jesus Christ our Lord.

does Paul's earlier description of the universality of sin in 1:18–3:20 and his intimation of the gift of conscience that provided a type of "law" that was violated. The insidious powers of Sin and Death were indeed ruling since the time of Adam.

At the end of 5:14, Paul makes an explicit connection between Adam and Jesus. In calling the former a "type of the one who was to come," he sets up the comparison he will make in the following verses. As Adam was a foundational figure and a representative of a way of being human that had lasting consequences, so now the same is true of Jesus, who reveals another way: the way of obedience to God. It is this way that leads to a "new creation" (2 Cor 5:17; Gal 6:15).

In its section on **original sin** (which relies on Romans 5), the *Catechism of the Catholic Church* recognizes that the transmission of sin from Adam to all human beings is a mystery: "How did the sin of Adam become the sin of all his descendants? The whole human race is in Adam 'as one body of one man' (Thomas Aquinas). By this 'unity of the human race' all . . . are implicated in Adam's sin, as all are implicated in Christ's justice. Still, the transmission of original sin is a mystery that we cannot fully understand" (404).

5:15-21 Grace and Life Through Christ

Paul now sets forth a stark contrast between two ways of being human and what follows from them. On the one hand, Adam's "transgression"—his disobedience to the divine command—led to several devastating consequences: the making of "sinners" of all who follow Adam's disobedience; judgment and condemnation; and death (both physical death and spiritual death, understood as separation from God, and the enslaving reign of Sin and Death). On the other hand, Jesus' "righteous act"—his giving over of his own life in self-giving love in obedience to God—has led to "acquittal" (i.e., the forgiveness of sins) and the end of the oppressive reign of Sin and Death. God's righteousness now reigns.

In 5:19 Paul states that it is through Jesus' obedience that "many will be made righteous." Observe the accent on Jesus' obedience, which is synonymous with his faithfulness. This statement bolsters our reading of 3:22 as referring to *Jesus' faithfulness* as the privileged revelation of God's righteousness, rather than the *human response* of faith in Christ. Jesus, the new Adam, manifests that obedience to God's will is what leads to life. Created in God's image and likeness, human beings are to reflect God's ways to others. We can do so because Jesus' obedience (his faithfulness) has transformative power: We are "made righteous," empowered to live and walk in his way of self-giving love.

This empowerment is from the Spirit, as Romans 8 will make clear.

At the end of the passage, Paul makes another reference to the Jewish law. Here he posits that the law came not to prevent trespasses but to *increase* them! We will have to wait until Romans 7 for his explanation of this enigmatic statement. For now, it is sufficient to appreciate that Jesus, the new Adam, has reversed and overcome Adam's disobedience and its devastating effects. Through Jesus' faithful obedience, grace—the gift of God's life and love—has proven to be more powerful than Sin and Death. This is good news indeed!

EXPLORING LESSON TWO

1. What are the two possible translations of *pistis Christou* (3:22)? Which one do you find more compelling and why?

2. What does "expiation" mean? What does the sacrificial death of Jesus accomplish, according to Paul (3:24-26)?

3. Paul is clear that we are "justified" (or brought into right relationship with God) by God's grace and Jesus' faithfulness, not by our own doing (3:27-31). Have you experienced this sheer grace in your own life? How have you been assured that you have been "justified"?

4. Read Genesis 12:1-9 and 15:1-6 alongside Romans 4. What promises did God make to Abraham (known here as Abram)? What was Abraham's response?

5. What is Paul's purpose in pointing out that Abraham had faith in God before he was circumcised (4:9-12)?

6. Have you ever felt that God was calling you to step out in faith, as Abraham did? What were the circumstances? Was God faithful to you as God was faithful to Abraham in Genesis?

7. Paul remarks on the maturing of faith through afflictions and endurance (5:1-5). Who in your life serves as an example of this mature faith and "proven character"? What do you most admire about them?

8. a) How is Jesus the new Adam (5:12-21)?

b) How do we as individuals participate in Adam's sin? How can we participate in Jesus' faithfulness?

9. Paul writes that, through Jesus, "where sin increased, grace overflowed all the more" (5:20-21). Does this ring true with your own experience? Where or how have you witnessed this reality of God's overflowing love?

10. What have you found most interesting in your study of Romans so far? What have you found the most challenging?

CLOSING PRAYER

Prayer

[T]he love of God has been poured out into our hearts through the holy Spirit that has been given to us. (Rom 5:5)

God of love and life, thank you for pouring into our hearts the gift of your love through the Holy Spirit. Help us always to appreciate this gift and to be open to the ways your Spirit transforms and empowers us. Help us to grow in obedience and faithfulness to you and your ways. We pray today especially for . . .

LESSON THREE

Romans 6–8

Begin your personal study and group discussion with a simple and sincere prayer such as:

Prayer

Loving God, send your Spirit upon us as we study the writings of your apostle Paul. Open our ears, our minds, and especially our hearts. Deepen your love within us, and transform us to embody and proclaim the good news you have revealed in your son Jesus Christ.

Read the Bible text of Romans 6–8, found in the outside columns of pages 48–56, highlighting what stands out to you.

Read the accompanying commentary to add to your understanding.

Respond to the questions on pages 57–59, Exploring Lesson Three.

The Closing Prayer on page 60 is for your personal use and may be used at the end of group discussion.

IV: Justification and the Christian Life

CHAPTER 6

Freedom from Sin; Life in God

1What then shall we say? Shall we persist in
sin that grace may abound? Of course not! 2How
can we who died to sin yet live in it? 3Or are you
unaware that we who were baptized into Christ
Jesus were baptized into his death? 4We were
indeed buried with him through baptism into
death, so that, just as Christ was raised from the
dead by the glory of the Father, we too might live
in newness of life.
5For if we have grown into union with him
through a death like his, we shall also be united
with him in the resurrection. 6We know that our
old self was crucified with him, so that our sinful
body might be done away with, that we might no
longer be in slavery to sin. 7For a dead person has
been absolved from sin. 8If, then, we have died
with Christ, we believe that we shall also live with
him. 9We know that Christ, raised from the dead,
dies no more; death no longer has power over
him. 10As to his death, he died to sin once and for
all; as to his life, he lives for God. 11Consequently,
you too must think of yourselves as [being] dead
to sin and living for God in Christ Jesus.

continue

JUSTIFICATION AND THE CHRISTIAN LIFE

Romans 6:1–8:39

6:1-23 Freedom from Sin; Life in God

Paul now begins to set forth the implications of the gospel proclamation for moral living. He gives voice to an imaginary interlocutor who raises objections and questions. These provide the structure for Romans 6–7 and are the type of misunderstandings that the apostle's teaching apparently provoked. He avails himself of the opportunity here to respond to them.

The first objection is: If grace abounds all the more where there is sin, why not keep on sinning so that grace might increase (see also 3:8)? (One can imagine the sophomore in the back of the classroom raising such a question!)

Paul finds this preposterous, and he responds by reminding the faithful in Rome about what took place in their baptism. Romans 6:1-11 is a particularly precious text because of what it teaches about Paul's understanding of baptism and, by extension, of the sacraments in general: They bring us into union with Jesus. In baptism, we died with Christ, sharing in his death and burial (the latter is probably an allusion to the practice of being fully submerged in the baptismal waters). By this "death," we are freed from the reign of Sin and Death that was unleashed by the disobedience of Adam.

Paul's language is dynamic. He explains that we are baptized *into* Christ Jesus. On one level, this points to the intimacy we have as individuals with Jesus. On another level, it refers to our entering into the Body of Christ, the community of believers that make up his Body (see Rom 12:5; 1 Cor 12:27). In this Body, the faithful are united with Jesus in his resurrection from the dead and are empowered (by the Spirit, as we will see) to "live in newness of life." No longer under the enslaving tyranny of Sin and Death, we can present ourselves and every part of our bodies (e.g., hands, tongues) for works of righteousness. That is, just as God's righteousness has been revealed through Jesus' self-giving love on the cross, so our works of righteousness are to participate in this dynamic of self-giving love. Just as Christ died once for all and now lives for God, we the baptized—freed from the reign of Sin and Death—are also to live for God, in faithfulness and obedience to God's ways.

In 6:14, Paul distinguishes between living "under grace" and "under the law." The latter expression is, for him, synonymous with "under Sin and Death." The reason for this will become clear as the passage unfolds.

The apostle then gives voice to another objection to his proclamation of the gospel: Since we are not under the law, why not keep sinning? The implication is that grace seems to give us license to do as we please. Paul responds by drawing on the notions of slavery and obedience to one's master. Paul's anthropology—that is, his understanding of what it means to be human—presumes that we live in service of someone or something bigger than ourselves. We like to think of ourselves as free and fully autonomous, but the reality is that, as creatures, that is not the case. Jesus expressed this truth as the choice between serving God or mammon (i.e., wealth; see Matt 6:24). A question we might ask ourselves is: What is the basic motivation for making the choices and decisions in my life? When we seek the ways of egoism and selfishness, and when we, like Adam, grasp after life where it is not offered to us by God, we become "slaves of sin." But when we are committed to God and God's ways, we become "slaves of God" and "slaves of righteousness." With these paradoxical expressions, Paul insists that this way of living is truly life-giving, because it is the way of life empowered by the Spirit and embodied by Jesus. Living this way, as we will see later in the letter, is to be truly free.

Next, Paul changes metaphors from slavery to wage-earning. The "wage" that Sin pays its subjects is death, including spiritual death (separation from God). Notice that God does not "pay" (a helpful reminder that God never "owes" us anything). Sanctification—the bestowal of the Spirit—is a "gift"; so, too, is "eternal life in Christ Jesus our Lord."

12Therefore, sin must not reign over your
mortal bodies so that you obey their desires.
13And do not present the parts of your bodies to
sin as weapons for wickedness, but present your-
selves to God as raised from the dead to life and
the parts of your bodies to God as weapons for
righteousness. 14For sin is not to have any power
over you, since you are not under the law but
under grace.

15What then? Shall we sin because we are not
under the law but under grace? Of course not!
16Do you not know that if you present yourselves
to someone as obedient slaves, you are slaves of
the one you obey, either of sin, which leads to
death, or of obedience, which leads to righteous-
ness? 17But thanks be to God that, although you
were once slaves of sin, you have become obedient
from the heart to the pattern of teaching to which
you were entrusted. 18Freed from sin, you have
become slaves of righteousness. 19I am speaking
in human terms because of the weakness of your
nature. For just as you presented the parts of your
bodies as slaves to impurity and to lawlessness for
lawlessness, so now present them as slaves to righ-
teousness for sanctification. 20For when you were
slaves of sin, you were free from righteousness.
21But what profit did you get then from the things
of which you are now ashamed? For the end of
those things is death. 22But now that you have
been freed from sin and have become slaves of
God, the benefit that you have leads to sanctifica-
tion, and its end is eternal life. 23For the wages of
sin is death, but the gift of God is eternal life in
Christ Jesus our Lord.

continue

7:1-6 Freedom from the Law

Up to this point, Paul has been making some cryptic allusions to the law. Now he starts to give some clarity to his position. He addresses himself to "people who know the

CHAPTER 7

Freedom from the Law

[1]Are you unaware, brothers (for I am speaking
to people who know the law), that the law has
jurisdiction over one as long as one lives? [2]Thus a
married woman is bound by law to her living hus-
band; but if her husband dies, she is released from
the law in respect to her husband. [3]Consequently,
while her husband is alive she will be called an
adulteress if she consorts with another man. But
if her husband dies she is free from that law, and
she is not an adulteress if she consorts with an-
other man.
[4]In the same way, my brothers, you also were
put to death to the law through the body of
Christ, so that you might belong to another, to
the one who was raised from the dead in order
that we might bear fruit for God. [5]For when we
were in the flesh, our sinful passions, awakened
by the law, worked in our members to bear fruit
for death. [6]But now we are released from the law,
dead to what held us captive, so that we may serve
in the newness of the spirit and not under the
obsolete letter.

continue

law"—that is, to the Jewish believers in Rome (and, perhaps, to some Gentile believers for whom the Jewish law had become important). He expresses a general principle—namely, that law has jurisdiction over those subject to it as long as these subjects are living. He then gives an example from Jewish law to illustrate the point. A Jewish woman was bound to her husband as long as he was alive. (Jewish women could not initiate divorce.) It was only upon the husband's death that she became "free" to marry another; otherwise, she would be guilty of adultery.

The apostle then claims that a "death" has occurred that has freed the Roman faithful from the Jewish law as the exclusive way of being God's covenant people. Whose death? The death of Jesus, in which they participated at their baptism. Having been raised with Christ, they are now free to belong to another. To whom? To the risen Christ! To be sure, Paul's analogy is far from perfect. But his meaning is easy enough to ascertain. A death has brought about the freedom to give one's full loyalty to another: to Jesus and not the law.

Two additional details warrant our attention. Paul's use of the analogy of marriage suggests an intimacy to which we are invited in our relationship with Jesus. And his reference to "bear[ing] fruit for God" is shorthand for the good we are called to do through the Spirit's empowerment. It is this empowerment by the Spirit that the apostle contrasts with "the obsolete letter" of the law. (Note that, while the NABRE does not, most translations capitalize "Spirit" in 7:6.)

7:7-12 Acquaintance with Sin Through the Law

Paul now deals with a third objection, likely spurred by what he wrote in 7:5—namely, that the law awakened in him "sinful passions." Is the law, then, sin? This is dangerous language, and Paul knows it. To associate the divinely given Jewish law with sin was tantamount to blasphemy for a Jew (including one like Paul, who was a Christ-believer). He initially answers strongly in the negative but then quickly concedes that the command "You shall not covet" did not prevent him from coveting; rather, it wakened covetousness within him. Paul's choice of citing this commandment is apt, because it culminates the Ten Commandments, and its being broken impacts adversely both the vertical (God–human) and horizontal (human–human) axes of covenant relationship.

The real problem, according to the apostle, is not the commandment itself but personified Sin that found an "opportunity" in the commandment to wreak havoc, producing in the heart various passions and temptations to sin, leading to death. In other words, the law became an unwitting accomplice of the malevolent power of Sin. Like the serpent in the garden, Sin acted by deceit, promising life where it is not offered. The extent of its evil is seen in that it could co-opt what is in fact "holy and righteous and good" (because the law is God-given)—something that promised life (see, e.g., Lev 18:5)—and turn it into the very opposite. Thus, he illustrates the extent of the evil power of Sin (and Death) from which we have been freed through Christ.

Regarding the law, what is implicit for Paul is that the problem is not the law in and of itself. The problem with the law is that, while it makes demands and commands, it does not—and cannot—provide the wherewithal and empowerment to fulfill and obey it. As we will see, this is something that only the Spirit can accomplish. Hence, the law on its own could only make known what is sinful (3:20). And because of the co-opting power of Sin, it increased trespasses (5:20).

7:13-25 Sin and Death

Paul expresses a fourth objection: Did the good (i.e., the law) become death for those who sinned? Here he makes explicit what was suggested above—namely, that his intention is to show Sin for what it is, as something wicked "beyond measure," bringing about death through the law that is itself good and spiritual.

The main exegetical issue in this passage is to determine to whom the pronoun "I" refers. A straightforward reading would seem to suggest the apostle himself, as though he is speaking autobiographically. But Paul's description of moral weakness and helplessness in these verses flies in the face of how he presents himself elsewhere (see, e.g., Phil 3:4-6, where he presents himself as steadfast in keeping the law). Rather, Paul is employing the literary device of speaking in character. That is, he takes on the persona of someone who is trapped by the enslaving power of Sin and Death (from which the apostle himself has already been redeemed). His presentation is dramatic, as he captures the desperation of one who is completely helpless (to modern ears, his description can even sound like one who is trapped in an addiction).

Acquaintance with Sin Through the Law

7What then can we say? That the law is sin? Of
course not! Yet I did not know sin except through
the law, and I did not know what it is to covet
except that the law said, "You shall not covet."
8But sin, finding an opportunity in the command-
ment, produced in me every kind of covetousness.
Apart from the law sin is dead. 9I once lived out-
side the law, but when the commandment came,
sin became alive; 10then I died, and the command-
ment that was for life turned out to be death for
me. 11For sin, seizing an opportunity in the com-
mandment, deceived me and through it put me
to death. 12So then the law is holy, and the com-
mandment is holy and righteous and good.

Sin and Death

13Did the good, then, become death for me?
Of course not! Sin, in order that it might be shown
to be sin, worked death in me through the good,
so that sin might become sinful beyond measure
through the commandment. 14We know that the
law is spiritual; but I am carnal, sold into slavery
to sin. 15What I do, I do not understand. For I do
not do what I want, but I do what I hate. 16Now if
I do what I do not want, I concur that the law is
good. 17So now it is no longer I who do it, but sin
that dwells in me. 18For I know that good does
not dwell in me, that is, in my flesh. The willing
is ready at hand, but doing the good is not. 19For
I do not do the good I want, but I do the evil I do
not want. 20Now if [I] do what I do not want, it
is no longer I who do it, but sin that dwells in me.
21So, then, I discover the principle that when I
want to do right, evil is at hand. 22For I take de-
light in the law of God, in my inner self, 23but I
see in my members another principle at war with
the law of my mind, taking me captive to the law
of sin that dwells in my members. 24Miserable one
that I am! Who will deliver me from this mortal
body? 25Thanks be to God through Jesus Christ
our Lord. Therefore, I myself, with my mind, serve
the law of God but, with my flesh, the law of sin.

continue

CHAPTER 8

The Flesh and the Spirit

[1]Hence, now there is no condemnation for those who are in Christ Jesus. [2]For the law of the spirit of life in Christ Jesus has freed you from the law of sin and death. [3]For what the law, weakened by the flesh, was powerless to do, this God has done: by sending his own Son in the likeness of sinful flesh and for the sake of sin, he condemned sin in the flesh, [4]so that the righteous decree of the law might be fulfilled in us, who live not according to the flesh but according to the spirit. [5]For those who live according to the flesh are concerned with the things of the flesh, but those who live according to the spirit with the things of the spirit. [6]The concern of the flesh is death, but the concern of the spirit is life and peace. [7]For the concern of the flesh is hostility toward God; it does not submit to the law of God, nor can it; [8]and those who are in the flesh cannot please God. [9]But you are not in the flesh; on the contrary, you are in the spirit, if only the Spirit of God dwells in you. Whoever does not have the Spirit of Christ does not belong to him. [10]But if Christ is in you, although the body is dead because of sin, the spirit is alive because of righteousness. [11]If the Spirit of the one who raised Jesus from the dead dwells in you, the one who raised Christ from the dead will give life to your mortal bodies also, through his Spirit that dwells in you. [12]Consequently, brothers, we are not debtors to the flesh, to live according to the flesh. [13]For if you live according to the flesh, you will die, but if by the spirit you put to death the deeds of the body, you will live.

continue

In 7:14, Paul introduces a distinction that is crucial for understanding both this passage and what he will say in Romans 8. On the one hand, he states that "the law is spiritual [*pneumatikos*]" because it is from God and is thus holy and good, as is the divine Spirit (*pneuma*). On the other hand, he refers to the "I" as "carnal" (*sarkinos*). This adjective is related to the noun *sarx* ("flesh"). Paul sometimes employs the term "flesh" in a neutral manner, to indicate that human existence is enfleshed (see, e.g., Gal 2:20). But more often than not, especially when he contrasts "flesh" with "Spirit," he uses it to signify human existence as perishable and subject to moral weakness. For Paul, human beings are either under the influence and empowerment of God's Spirit or not. Without the presence and help of the Spirit, they are like the "I" described in the present passage: unable to do the good they want to do and know is right, and prone to doing what they know is not life-giving. This is truly a divided self, a person in whom Sin (and not the Spirit) dwells. Although Paul does not explain how such persons are morally responsible, he presumes that they are (likely because of initial acts of disobedience, after the pattern of Adam, to God and God's ways).

At the end of his dramatization of the carnal "I," Paul cries out in character: "Miserable one that I am! Who will deliver me from this mortal body?" He then interjects with good news: He gives thanks to God for acting through Jesus' loving act of redemption, which has freed us from the enslaving power of Sin.

8:1-13 The Flesh and the Spirit

Paul continues his proclamation of the good news, the revelation of God's righteousness, focusing now on the gift of the Holy Spirit. Romans 8 is the most extended treatment of God's Spirit in the New Testament, and we can be grateful to Paul for what he teaches here. (An important note: Though the NABRE does not consistently capitalize "spirit" throughout this passage and the rest of the chapter, Paul is referring to *God's* Spirit throughout. Therefore, "Spirit" will be capitalized in this commentary on Romans 8, even in direct quotations where the NABRE uses the lowercase "spirit.")

By Jesus becoming human (i.e., taking on "flesh" in the neutral sense) and through his faithfulness-unto-death on the cross, God condemned personified Sin. This is a manifestation of divine righteousness and justice, as it is something that only God could do. Freed from the ways Sin co-opted the law, and now empowered by the Spirit, the faithful can fulfill "the righteous decree of the law."

Here is an important point! Like Jesus with the Jewish law, Paul does not throw out the baby with the bathwater. Both Jesus and Paul focus on what constitutes the heart or essence of the law: our love for God expressed especially—if not solely—by love of neighbor. Both Jesus and Paul call this the fulfillment of the law (see Rom 13:8; Luke 10:36-37). It is only by living by the Spirit's empowerment that we can fulfill the law in this manner, thereby experiencing "life and peace." Indeed, we will know the fullness of resurrection of life because this Spirit is the same one who raised Jesus from the dead. Those who live "according to the flesh"—that is, without the Spirit's aid—cannot please God, for "flesh" in this sense is hostile to God, rebelling against God and God's ways. This is because flesh, understood in the negative sense, tends toward death.

Before proceeding to the next passage, it will be helpful to point out the fluidity of Paul's language about the Spirit. He refers to "the Spirit," "the Spirit of God," and "the Spirit of Christ," all pointing to the same (Holy) Spirit. In addition, he uses the phrase "Christ . . . in you" synonymously with the Spirit's indwelling (8:10). That is, Christ is present within us through the abiding presence of the Holy Spirit, the gift of God's love poured into our hearts (see 5:5).

Children of God Through Adoption

[14]For those who are led by the Spirit of God are children of God. [15]For you did not receive a spirit of slavery to fall back into fear, but you received a spirit of adoption, through which we cry, "Abba, Father!" [16]The Spirit itself bears witness with our spirit that we are children of God, [17]and if children, then heirs, heirs of God and joint heirs with Christ, if only we suffer with him so that we may also be glorified with him.

continue

8:14-17 Children of God Through Adoption

Paul next explains how the gift of the Spirit gives us a new identity: We are God's children through the "spirit of adoption." Adoption was commonplace in the apostle's time. One who was adopted attained the full rights and privileges of family members, including the right of inheritance.

The Spirit frees us from the tyranny of fear and slavery that marks the reign of Sin and Death. Instead, it is characterized by freedom and love. Moreover, as God's adopted children,

Paul frequently contrasts **flesh and spirit** (see Rom 8:5-9; 1 Cor 3:1-3; Gal 5:16-23). For Paul, "flesh" refers to all that is finite and corruptible. "Spirit" at times means the Holy Spirit but at other times represents that aspect of human existence that transcends what is finite. The contrast in these concepts can be summarized as follows:

Flesh	Spirit
All that is corrupt and fleeting	All that is permanent
That which is earthly (below)	That which is heavenly (above)
Leads to death	Leads to new life
Displeases God	Pleases God
Exhibited in a host of sinful activities	Exhibited in a host of virtues

Destiny of Glory

[18]I consider that the sufferings of this present time are as nothing compared with the glory to be revealed for us. [19]For creation awaits with eager expectation the revelation of the children of God; [20]for creation was made subject to futility, not of its own accord but because of the one who subjected it, in hope [21]that creation itself would be set free from slavery to corruption and share in the glorious freedom of the children of God. [22]We know that all creation is groaning in labor pains even until now; [23]and not only that, but we ourselves, who have the firstfruits of the Spirit, we also groan within ourselves as we wait for adoption, the redemption of our bodies. [24]For in hope we were saved. Now hope that sees for itself is not hope. For who hopes for what one sees? [25]But if we hope for what we do not see, we wait with endurance.

[26]In the same way, the Spirit too comes to the aid of our weakness; for we do not know how to pray as we ought, but the Spirit itself intercedes with inexpressible groanings. [27]And the one who searches hearts knows what is the intention of the Spirit, because it intercedes for the holy ones according to God's will.

continue

we can call out to God as "Abba, Father." This detail ought not to be passed over too quickly. This is how Jesus himself, in his life and ministry, called out to and related to God (see Mark 14:36). *Abba* connotes great intimacy between child and father. A healthy image of God is a loving parent. Indeed, at Jesus' baptism, he experienced God's calling him "beloved Son" as well as an outpouring of the Spirit that launched him into his ministry (Mark 1:9-11). Similarly, at our baptism we are adopted as God's beloved children and given the Spirit. Of course, there's a difference between Jesus and us. What he was by nature (God's Son, conceived by the Holy Spirit; see Luke 1:35), we are by adoption. This identity gives us a dignity we should always appreciate. It also calls and challenges us to recognize the dignity of others, who are fellow children of God. What a difference such recognition would make in our own families, communities, and world.

While it would be nice to end on this uplifting note, Paul teaches that to be adopted into the family of God also entails suffering, specifically suffering *with* Jesus. Here Paul refers to joining our sufferings to those of Jesus; to growing in self-giving love, which can require great sacrifice; and to suffering on account of the gospel.

8:18-27 Destiny of Glory

As was the case with Jesus, our suffering does not have the last word. It leads to glory: the glory of resurrected life (the inheritance to which Paul refers). This will be the full realization of the kingdom of God and the new creation (as suggested by the imagery of a woman in birth pangs; see 8:22).

While it is natural for us to think of this realization exclusively in terms of the transformation of human life, Paul reminds us that the fullness of God's salvation also includes the transformation of the created order. It was this connection that led Pope Francis to continually remind us of the call to care for our common home, in preparation for this transformation. Just as our hearts groan for the fullness of salvation (think of St. Augustine's famous saying about our hearts being restless until they rest in God), so too is creation groaning until God brings about this restoration and transformation. The groaning of creation is an allusion to the story in Genesis 2–3, where Adam's disobedience also led to consequences for nature.

The God who raised Jesus from the dead is the source of our hope. Indeed, the gift of the Spirit is a foretaste, the "firstfruits" of the fullness of the life to come and a pledge from God that grounds our hope and gives us endurance as we await and pray "thy kingdom come."

A word of clarification about Romans 8:23, where Paul speaks of adoption and redemption as future realities: Here we get a sense of what theologians refer to as the "already but not yet" quality of Paul's understanding of salvation. While we have already been adopted through the Spirit and have already been redeemed from the enslaving powers of Sin and Death, we still await the full realization of these gifts of God.

It is not just human hearts and creation that are groaning; so too is the Spirit of God, who groans with "inexpressible groanings"! What Paul says here is very important for our prayer lives. Most of us have had periods in our lives when our prayer is dry and God seems distant. But Paul teaches that the Spirit is always interceding on our behalf. The Spirit is thus not only God-*within*-us (as mentioned in our discussion of 5:5); the Spirit is also God-*for*-us, advocating for us in a way that God, who knows human hearts, understands. Notice how the apostle describes how the Spirit prays: "according to God's will." This should be very consoling to us, who are called to faithfulness and obedience to God and God's ways. This is the way Jesus, the new Adam, prayed (see, e.g., Mark 14:36: "not what I will but what you will"). Again, the Spirit leads us into living in the new creation.

Predestination is the theological notion that God's sovereign plan of salvation directs the unfolding of history in due course. Different explanations of this concept have evolved over time.
In Paul's thought, predestination in no way interferes with free will. We always remain free to accept or reject God's offer of eternal salvation. Paradoxically, binding ourselves to Jesus Christ frees us to live a just life in accordance with God's plan. Yet to be predestined means to be oriented toward salvation from the beginning. This is God's will: All are chosen so that all might be saved (see 1 Tim 2:4).

God's Indomitable Love in Christ

28We know that all things work for good for
those who love God, who are called according to
his purpose. 29For those he foreknew he also pre-
destined to be conformed to the image of his Son,
so that he might be the firstborn among many
brothers. 30And those he predestined he also
called; and those he called he also justified; and
those he justified he also glorified.

31What then shall we say to this? If God is for
us, who can be against us? 32He who did not spare
his own Son but handed him over for us all, how
will he not also give us everything else along with
him? 33Who will bring a charge against God's
chosen ones? It is God who acquits us. 34Who will
condemn? It is Christ [Jesus] who died, rather,
was raised, who also is at the right hand of God,
who indeed intercedes for us. 35What will separate
us from the love of Christ? Will anguish, or dis-
tress, or persecution, or famine, or nakedness, or
peril, or the sword? 36As it is written:

> "For your sake we are being slain all the day;
> we are looked upon as sheep to be
> slaughtered."

37No, in all these things we conquer over-
whelmingly through him who loved us. 38For I
am convinced that neither death, nor life, nor
angels, nor principalities, nor present things, nor
future things, nor powers, 39nor height, nor depth,
nor any other creature will be able to separate us
from the love of God in Christ Jesus our Lord.

8:28-39 God's Indomitable Love in Christ

Paul starts to bring his treatment of the Spirit to a conclusion by commenting that God works all things for good for those who love God (a preferred rendering over that of the NABRE, as the focus should be on what *God* does). He then alludes to the divine plan of forming a covenant people, the Jew and Gentile family of faith promised to Abraham. As was the case with the Isaian servant before he was in his mother's womb (see Isa 49:1), God foreknew those whom he foreordained "to be conformed to the image of his Son." ("Foreordained" is a better word than "predestined" here, as it allows for the human freedom needed to respond to God with obedience, while "predestined" is sometimes interpreted as a future already set in stone.) Here Paul leaves implicit that it is the Spirit who transforms people into the image of Jesus, something he makes explicit elsewhere (see, e.g., 2 Cor 3:18). Being conformed to Jesus' image empowers believers to embody his ways of self-giving love by which he revealed God's love in both his life and his death.

Notice the imagery of family in 8:29. Jesus is described as the "firstborn" of many brothers and sisters, the members of the family of faith that God is forming among Jewish and Gentile believers. They are then to take on what we would call the "family likeness," which is self-giving love after the example of Jesus. These are the ones whom God calls, makes righteous ("justifie[s]"), and will ultimately glorify. Again, it is crucial to recall the importance of covenant for Paul. God, through the Spirit, is forming a people to show forth God's ways of love.

It is this divine love that the apostle trumpets in the final verses of this section. To be sure, he has already sounded this theme, starting with the mention of God's love poured into our hearts through the gift of the Spirit (5:5) and continuing with the "proof" of God's love as demonstrated by Jesus' dying for us when we were most in need of salvation (5:6-10). Now, with a series of rhetorical questions, Paul highlights this love in exhilarating fashion. The fundamental point is to make clear that God is "for us"—always at and on our side. This is an essential aspect of God's righteousness or God's covenant faithfulness. We have already touched upon one way God reveals the extent of divine love in that God did not spare God's only Son. Whereas faithful Abraham was *willing* to sacrifice his only son (see Gen 22), God *actually put forth* Jesus as expiation for sins through his faithful death (3:25). Having been justified (acquitted from sin and made members of God's covenant people), nothing—not even death itself—can separate us from God's love. Indeed, Jesus now intercedes for us at God's right hand, another manifestation of God being "for us."

Paul's closing citation of Psalm 44 (see 8:36) functions to acknowledge that, like Jesus, the faithful may encounter opposition and even persecution (such as those listed in 8:35). Notably, however, the psalm concludes with a prayer to God to redeem believers in God's mercy (Ps 44:27), an allusion to God's covenant love.

Prayer Starter: What if we lived as though we truly believed that nothing can separate us from the love of God? What might our lives be like if we consciously walked through each day with this awareness? Intentionally live in the shelter of God's love this week.

EXPLORING LESSON THREE

1. a) What is something new you learned about baptism by reading Romans 6 and the accompanying commentary?

   b) What does it mean to you to have "died with Christ" (6:8) or—in even more graphic language—to have your "old self . . . crucified with him" (6:6)?

2. In Romans 6, Paul responds to objections he has heard about his gospel message. What is one of these objections, and what is Paul's basic response?

3. What analogy does Paul use in Romans 7:1-7 to explain how believers are released from the law?

4. If the law increases sinful passions (7:5-11), how can Paul say that it is "holy and righteous and good" (7:12)?

5. a) What reason does the commentary give for suggesting that Paul was not speaking about himself when he describes the struggle with sin in 7:13-25?

   b) What about this passage (7:13-25) do you find most relatable or inspiring?

6. What does Paul mean by the term "flesh" (*sarx*) in Romans 7–8?

7. What is the relationship between Christ and the Spirit as described in Romans 8:1-13?

8. What does it mean that believers, as children of God in the Spirit, have the privilege of calling God "Abba" just as Jesus did (8:15)?

9. The commentary describes the "already but not yet" tension that we find in 8:18-27. How have you experienced this tension in your own spiritual life? What gifts from God do you already have, and what gifts or experiences do you still yearn for?

10. Paul ends Romans 8 with a powerful declaration that absolutely nothing can separate us from God's love (8:35-39). What proof or assurance does Paul offer for this (see 8:32)?

CLOSING PRAYER

If God is for us, who can be against us?
(Rom 8:31)

Abba, Father, thank you for the many ways you show your love to us, your beloved children. Help us to grow in faithful trust in you, knowing that your Spirit of love dwells within us and that you show us the way to life through your Son Jesus. Protect us from fear and anxiety, and help us to bear witness with joy to your love. We pray today especially for . . .

LESSON FOUR

Romans 9–11

Begin your personal study and group discussion with a simple and sincere prayer such as:

Prayer

Loving God, send your Spirit upon us as we study the writings of your apostle Paul. Open our ears, our minds, and especially our hearts. Deepen your love within us, and transform us to embody and proclaim the good news you have revealed in your son Jesus Christ.

Read the Bible text of Romans 9–11, found in the outside columns of pages 62–71, highlighting what stands out to you.

Read the accompanying commentary to add to your understanding.

Respond to the questions on pages 72–74, Exploring Lesson Four.

The Closing Prayer on page 75 is for your personal use and may be used at the end of group discussion.

V: Jews and Gentiles in God's Plan

CHAPTER 9

Paul's Love for Israel

[1]I speak the truth in Christ, I do not lie; my
conscience joins with the holy Spirit in bearing
me witness [2]that I have great sorrow and constant
anguish in my heart. [3]For I could wish that I my-
self were accursed and separated from Christ for
the sake of my brothers, my kin according to the
flesh. [4]They are Israelites; theirs the adoption, the
glory, the covenants, the giving of the law, the
worship, and the promises; [5]theirs the patriarchs,
and from them, according to the flesh, is the Mes-
siah. God who is over all be blessed forever. Amen.

continue

JEWS AND GENTILES IN GOD'S PLAN

Romans 9:1–11:36

Following his triumphant declaration of God's love at the end of Romans 8, Paul now offers a lengthy *apologia*, or defense, for God's righteousness and righteous ways.

Why did the apostle feel the need to defend God, and for the length of three chapters at that? Several intertwining dynamics are at play here. While the proclamation of the gospel led to fruitful results, the fact of the matter is that, for the most part, Gentiles were more likely than Jews to respond to it with faith. Many Jews found the notion of a crucified Messiah to be a serious stumbling block. Indeed, Deuteronomy 21:23 declares that anyone hanged on a tree is cursed by God (see Gal 3:13 for Paul's response). Even Jesus' first disciples struggled with the idea that the Messiah must suffer and die (see, e.g., Mark 8:31-33).

The largely Jewish rejection of the gospel—along with Gentile acceptance of it—led to some difficult questions. Given Israel's prominent role in God's relationship with humankind, has God now rejected God's people, the Jews? Or, as Paul will express the matter in 9:6, has God's word failed? Have the Gentile faithful replaced the Jews in God's plan? Paul will address some of these questions in the texts that follow.

9:1-5 Paul's Love for Israel

These were not mere academic questions for Paul; they were personal. The (largely) Jewish rejection of the gospel pained him, causing him "great sorrow" and heartfelt "anguish." Notice that Paul still regarded himself as a Jew (albeit as one who was a Christ-believer), and he still considered Jews to be his kin. His love and concern for them were such that he was even willing to be considered "accursed and separated from Christ" if it meant that his Jewish brothers and sisters would come to accept the gospel with faith. In this, he imitated Moses' willingness to be cut off from God's people if that meant God would forgive them after the golden calf incident (see Exod 32:31-32).

Paul then sets forth a list of Israel's privileges and blessings. (These are in addition to the "utterances of God" mentioned in 3:2.) Paul begins the list by using the honorific title "Israelites" (see Gen 32:29). The reference to "adoption" alludes to their special relationship with God (e.g., Exod 4:22). "Glory" points to divine manifestations to the people, such as at Sinai and as God led them through the wilderness. The "covenants" were made with

Abraham, Moses, and David. The "law" is that given to Moses at Sinai, when God entered into covenant with the people. An important part of this law was the cultic regulations concerning how to "worship" God in the temple cult. The "promises" of a countless progeny and land (recall our discussion of the Abraham story in Rom 4) were made to the "patriarchs" (Abraham, Isaac, and Jacob). As we will see, these promises culminated with the coming of Jesus the "Messiah." All of these blessings and privileges, the apostle insists, are real and enduring. They testify to God's love for the Jews.

Translators have to decide how to render the final blessing (9:5). Like most translations, the NABRE puts a full stop after "Messiah" and then has Paul offer a blessing to God. The more natural way to read the Greek text, however, is "the Messiah who is over all, God blessed forever." If the latter is correct (and I think it is), it marks the only place where Paul directly calls Jesus "God." However, given Jesus' role in the revelation of God's love and righteousness, this declaration ought not to be surprising. Jesus is truly and uniquely the personal expression of God.

9:6-24 God's Free Choice

In 9:6-29, Paul offers what is, in effect, a retelling of God's dealings with Israel. He focuses on the distant past, alluding to incidents involving the patriarchs, then to the exodus, and next he cites passages from the prophetic corpus (from the time of the exile).

It is important to point out that the apostle's way of reading the scriptural texts here might strike some of us, at times, as unusual and even arbitrary. But to be fair to him, he was not trained in historical approaches that are used today. Paul was committed to reading the Scriptures not as something that pertained solely to the past but as a *living* word that still speaks to today's context. Moreover, he saw that God's ways have been consistent, and that God's character is righteous and merciful. He also discerned an overarching storyline that has culminated with the coming of Jesus the Messiah.

God's Free Choice

[6]But it is not that the word of God has failed. For not all who are of Israel are Israel, [7]nor are they all children of Abraham because they are his descendants; but "It is through Isaac that descendants shall bear your name." [8]This means that it is not the children of the flesh who are the children of God, but the children of the promise are counted as descendants. [9]For this is the wording of the promise, "About this time I shall return and Sarah will have a son." [10]And not only that, but also when Rebecca had conceived children by one husband, our father Isaac— [11]before they had yet been born or had done anything, good or bad, in order that God's elective plan might continue, [12]not by works but by his call—she was told, "The older shall serve the younger." [13]As it is written ". . . :

"I loved Jacob
but hated Esau."

[14]What then are we to say? Is there injustice on the part of God? Of course not! [15]For he says to Moses:

"I will show mercy to whom I will,
I will take pity on whom I will."

[16]So it depends not upon a person's will or exertion, but upon God, who shows mercy. [17]For the scripture says to Pharaoh, "This is why I have raised you up, to show my power through you that my name may be proclaimed throughout the earth." [18]Consequently, he has mercy upon whom he wills, and he hardens whom he wills.

[19]You will say to me then, "Why [then] does he still find fault? For who can oppose his will?" [20]But who indeed are you, a human being, to talk back to God? Will what is made say to its maker, "Why have you created me so?" [21]Or does not the potter have a right over the clay, to make out of the same lump one vessel for a noble purpose and another for an ignoble one? [22]What if God, wishing to show his wrath and make known his power, has endured with much patience the vessels of

continue

wrath made for destruction? 23This was to make
known the riches of his glory to the vessels of
mercy, which he has prepared previously for glory,
24namely, us whom he has called, not only from
the Jews but also from the Gentiles.

Witness of the Prophets

25As indeed he says in Hosea

"Those who were not my people I will call
'my people,'
and her who was not beloved I will call
'beloved.'
26And in the very place where it was said to
them, 'You are not my people,'
there they shall be called children of the
living God.

27And Isaiah cries out concerning Israel, "Though
the number of the Israelites were like the sand of
the sea, only a remnant will be saved; 28for deci-
sively and quickly will the Lord execute sentence
upon the earth." 29And as Isaiah predicted:

"Unless the Lord of hosts had left us
descendants,
we would have become like Sodom
and have been made like Gomorrah."

continue

In what follows, I will highlight Paul's main claims. Readers who want more details on the scriptural texts from which Paul draws and on how he adapts them in his retelling of God's dealings with Israel are encouraged to look at more detailed commentaries.

In the present passage, Paul highlights characteristics of God. God's outreach to certain individuals has been termed "merciful election." No one merits, on their own, to be chosen. Out of divine love, God has elected certain persons—and this is an important point—for the sake of forming a people, the Jew and Gentile family of faith. God is free to do as God sees fit. For instance, God is not beholden to cultural constraints that favored the elder son (9:12-13). Nor is it simply a matter of physical descent when it comes to election. Not all of Abraham's descendants became his "children" in the sense of God fulfilling the divine promises through them. What constitutes membership in the family of Abraham is a trusting, enduring response of faith to what God has revealed and promised. For Paul, this means responding in faith to what God has revealed and promised *through Jesus*. Paul's exploration of this dynamic speaks to the reality that, at the time this letter was written, many Jews were not accepting the gospel proclamation.

Paul's quotation of Malachi 1:3 in Romans 9:13 is not a statement of God's literal hatred for Esau or anyone else. In Jewish usage, "to hate" can mean "to love less," which is more about *priority* than about literal love or hate (compare, for example, Luke 14:26 and Matt 10:37). Paul is using this verse's figure of speech to refer to **God's election of Jacob** (unexpected, since Jacob was the younger twin) as an example of God's freedom to choose as God wills for the sake of the divine plan.

Paul's allusion to the exodus story and its aftermath makes two points. First, divine mercy trumps strict justice. When the Israelites immediately broke the covenant by making and worshiping the golden calf, the covenant was, for all intents and purposes, finished. But God showed mercy on the people and renewed the covenant. However, and second, God hardened the heart of Pharaoh and did not show him mercy. This can seem arbitrary and unfair. Yet, as Paul points out, God is sovereign. It is not the role of creatures to call into question God's purposes (just as the pot of clay has no right to complain to the potter). The allusion to Pharaoh's hardened heart—and the liberation of the Hebrews that followed—anticipates a point to be made at the end of Romans 9–11:

namely, that the hardening of Israel's hearts to the gospel led to the gospel being proclaimed, with great success, to the Gentiles.

Paul's explanations in this regard may not be fully satisfying to us. But they are a clear indication that Paul was wrestling with the issue of Jewish acceptance of the gospel on not only a theological but a personal level. Despite his personal disappointment that not all of his Jewish brothers and sisters accepted Jesus as the Messiah, Paul believed that God had a plan for both Jews and Gentiles. But he was the first to admit that God's ways are not our ways (see Isa 55:8).

9:25-29 Witness of the Prophets

Paul concludes this section (9:6-29) by citing the prophets Isaiah and Hosea. In the original context of these passages, Isaiah warned Israel against putting its trust in military alliances rather than in God, and Hosea reproved the people for idolatry. The apostle employs these texts to make two key points. In terms of Isaiah, though Israel eventually was led to exile, a faithful remnant remained behind. As we'll see, the notion of a faithful remnant will play an important role in Paul's presentation of those Jews who have responded favorably to the gospel. In terms of Hosea, God called back those who were named "not my people" (i.e., unfaithful Israel) and reinstated them as God's children. The apostle reads this text as prophesying what was happening with the Gentiles. Though formerly alienated from God, many were becoming God's children, being adopted through baptism into the family of faith.

9:30–10:21 Righteousness Based on Faith

Paul's retelling of the story of God and Israel now turns to the present context. In 9:30-33, he succinctly expresses where things stand. On the one hand, the Gentiles, who were not even seeking righteousness, have found the "righteousness that comes from faith"—that is, the righteousness that is manifested in Jesus' faithfulness-unto-death and received through

Righteousness Based on Faith

[30]What then shall we say? That Gentiles, who did not pursue righteousness, have achieved it, that is, righteousness that comes from faith; [31]but that Israel, who pursued the law of righteousness, did not attain to that law? [32]Why not? Because they did it not by faith, but as if it could be done by works. They stumbled over the stone that causes stumbling, [33]as it is written:

"Behold, I am laying a stone in Zion
that will make people stumble
and a rock that will make them fall,
and whoever believes in him shall not be put
to shame."

CHAPTER 10

[1]Brothers, my heart's desire and prayer to God on their behalf is for salvation. [2]I testify with regard to them that they have zeal for God, but it is not discerning. [3]For, in their unawareness of the righteousness that comes from God and their attempt to establish their own [righteousness], they did not submit to the righteousness of God. [4]For Christ is the end of the law for the justification of everyone who has faith.

[5]Moses writes about the righteousness that comes from [the] law, "The one who does these things will live by them." [6]But the righteousness that comes from faith says, "Do not say in your heart, 'Who will go up into heaven?' (that is, to bring Christ down) [7]or 'Who will go down into the abyss?' (that is, to bring Christ up from the dead)." [8]But what does it say?

"The word is near you, in your mouth and in your heart" (that is, the word of faith that we preach), [9]for, if you confess with your mouth that Jesus is Lord and believe in your heart that God raised him from the dead, you will be saved. [10]For one believes with the heart and so is justified, and one confesses with the mouth and so is saved. [11]For the scripture says, "No one who believes in him will be put to shame." [12]For there is no distinction between Jew and Greek; the same Lord

continue

is Lord of all, enriching all who call upon him.
[13]For "everyone who calls on the name of the Lord
will be saved."
[14]But how can they call on him in whom they
have not believed? And how can they believe in
him of whom they have not heard? And how can
they hear without someone to preach? [15]And how
can people preach unless they are sent? As it is
written, "How beautiful are the feet of those who
bring [the] good news!" [16]But not everyone has
heeded the good news; for Isaiah says, "Lord, who
has believed what was heard from us?" [17]Thus
faith comes from what is heard, and what is heard
comes through the word of Christ. [18]But I ask,
did they not hear? Certainly they did; for

"Their voice has gone forth to all the earth,
and their words to the ends of the world."

[19]But I ask, did not Israel understand? First Moses
says:

"I will make you jealous of those who are not
a nation;
with a senseless nation I will make you
angry."

[20]Then Isaiah speaks boldly and says:

"I was found [by] those who were not
seeking me;
I revealed myself to those who were not
asking for me."

[21]But regarding Israel he says, "All day long I
stretched out my hands to a disobedient and con-
tentious people."

continue

a faithful response to the gospel proclamation. The Jews, who were pursuing righteousness that "could be done by works [of law]," did not attain it. The apostle then cites two verses from Isaiah (Isa 28:16; 8:14) that refer to a "stone that causes stumbling" (or a "stumbling block" [*skandalon*]). This is an allusion to Messiah (Christ) Jesus, whose death on the cross was a "scandal" (the meaning of the Greek word) for many Jews.

Paul goes on to reiterate his love for his people. His heartfelt desire is for their salvation. He acknowledges that, as was the case with himself as a younger man (see, e.g., Gal 1:14), they have great "zeal for God, but it is not discerning." Rather than submit to God's righteousness as revealed through Jesus, they have insisted, in effect, on establishing their own righteousness. To be clear, this was not an attempt by Jews to "earn" salvation but an expression of their understanding of what they believed God wanted of them. Recalling Paul's life prior to his encounter with the risen Christ may be helpful here. Paul considered himself to be "blameless" according to the law (Phil 3:6). It was only after his encounter with the risen Christ that he came to believe that Jesus himself (and his faithfulness-unto-death) is the definitive source of righteousness.

In 10:4, Paul then offers a very important principle, one that is often misunderstood today. The NABRE reads, "Christ is the end of the law." What, precisely, is meant by the terms "end" and "law" in this sentence? For many commentators, Paul is saying that, with the coming of Jesus, the relevance of the Jewish law has come to a terminal end point. While the Greek word *telos* can have that meaning, it can also mean "end" in the sense of a "goal," thereby indicating a process that is leading to something that brings completion. And while the Greek word *nomos* can mean "law" in the sense of the Jewish law with its commandments, it can also refer to the first five books of the Bible that contain the law (i.e., the Pentateuch, or Torah). Moreover, Paul may be employing *nomos* (law) as a synecdoche, which means using a part to refer to the whole. That is, *nomos* (law) may refer to the Jewish Scriptures as a whole. The apostle's meaning is best captured thus: The Messiah is the climax (or culmination) of the story of Scripture, the goal toward which the whole story has been moving. As such, as the definitive revelation of God's righteousness, Jesus is the means of "justification"—of being brought into right relationship with God and others—for everyone who responds with faith to the gospel.

To illustrate his claim that Christ is the climax of Scripture, Paul offers a bold interpretation of Deuteronomy 30:12-14. The original setting of this passage was Moses' exhortation to Israel as they were about to enter the land promised to them. Moses taught the people that the law—the God-given means for their salvation—was not far from them at all. They don't have to climb the heavens or descend into the abyss to look for this law, because God has placed it in their hearts. But notice what Paul does here. He changes the source of the God-given means for salvation from the law to Jesus. *Jesus* is the one who, through his incarnation, came down from heaven. He is now raised from the dead (i.e., from "the abyss"). Hence, in the apostle's reading, it is Moses, the giver of the law, who testifies that God's righteousness comes through faith—the faithfulness of Jesus! This calls for a response of faith on the part of those who hear the gospel. They can so respond because God has sent messengers (apostles) like Paul to bring the good news to them in fulfillment of Isaiah 52:7 (see Rom 10:15). Moreover, God has poured the Spirit into their hearts (5:5). It is by the confession of faith and its embodiment in self-giving love that people—the Jew and Gentile family of faith—are saved by the one Lord, who is the revelation of divine righteousness.

According to Paul, the Jewish Scriptures also foretell Gentile acceptance as well as (the largely) Jewish rejection of the gospel. In 10:16, the apostle cites Isaiah 53:1: "Lord, who has believed what was heard from us?" Tellingly, this line is taken from the fourth Isaian Servant Song (Isa 52:13–53:12), which Paul understood as prophesying Jesus' salvific suffering. The lack of faithful response alluded to in the text pertains, for Paul, to the present situation of the proclamation of the gospel to Jews. He then cites Isaiah 65:1-2 as foretelling two things: (1) God has been found by a people not seeking God (i.e., the Gentiles); and (2) God has reached out to Israel, whose response is disobedience and contention (10:20-21).

CHAPTER 11

The Remnant of Israel

1I ask, then, has God rejected his people? Of
course not! For I too am an Israelite, a descendant
of Abraham, of the tribe of Benjamin. 2God has
not rejected his people whom he foreknew. Do
you not know what the scripture says about Elijah,
how he pleads with God against Israel? 3"Lord,
they have killed your prophets, they have torn
down your altars, and I alone am left, and they are
seeking my life." 4But what is God's response to
him? "I have left for myself seven thousand men
who have not knelt to Baal." 5So also at the present
time there is a remnant, chosen by grace. 6But if
by grace, it is no longer because of works; other-
wise grace would no longer be grace.

7What then? What Israel was seeking it did
not attain, but the elect attained it; the rest were
hardened, 8as it is written:

"God gave them a spirit of deep sleep,
eyes that should not see
and ears that should not hear,
down to this very day."

9And David says:

"Let their table become a snare and a trap,
a stumbling block and a retribution for them;
10let their eyes grow dim so that they may not see,
and keep their backs bent forever."

continue

11:1-10 The Remnant of Israel

Given this bleak situation that Paul faced in the present (i.e., the largely Jewish rejection of the gospel), he asks whether God has in turn rejected the Jews, whom Paul still understands to be God's people (11:1). The apostle insists that God has done no such thing. In fact, Paul holds himself up as an example. As a Benjamite (i.e., a member of the tribe of Benjamin and, therefore, a full-fledged member of the Jewish people) and "a descendant of Abraham," the

The Gentiles' Salvation

11Hence I ask, did they stumble so as to fall?
Of course not! But through their transgression
salvation has come to the Gentiles, so as to make
them jealous. 12Now if their transgression is en-
richment for the world, and if their diminished
number is enrichment for the Gentiles, how much
more their full number.

13Now I am speaking to you Gentiles. Inasmuch
then as I am the apostle to the Gentiles, I glory in
my ministry 14in order to make my race jealous
and thus save some of them. 15For if their rejection
is the reconciliation of the world, what will their
acceptance be but life from the dead? 16If the first-
fruits are holy, so is the whole batch of dough;
and if the root is holy, so are the branches.

17But if some of the branches were broken off,
and you, a wild olive shoot, were grafted in their
place and have come to share in the rich root of
the olive tree, 18do not boast against the branches.
If you do boast, consider that you do not support
the root; the root supports you. 19Indeed you will
say, "Branches were broken off so that I might be
grafted in." 20That is so. They were broken off be-
cause of unbelief, but you are there because of
faith. So do not become haughty, but stand in awe.
21For if God did not spare the natural branches,
[perhaps] he will not spare you either. 22See, then,
the kindness and severity of God: severity toward
those who fell, but God's kindness to you, pro-
vided you remain in his kindness; otherwise you
too will be cut off. 23And they also, if they do not
remain in unbelief, will be grafted in, for God is
able to graft them in again. 24For if you were cut
from what is by nature a wild olive tree, and
grafted, contrary to nature, into a cultivated one,
how much more will they who belong to it by
nature be grafted back into their own olive tree.

continue

apostle is part of the "remnant" of Jews who have responded with faith to the gospel proclamation. He is therefore living proof that God has not rejected God's people.

Paul then alludes to the story of the prophet Elijah told in 1 Kings 19:1-8. The original context was that Israel was living in apostasy, having chosen to worship the god Baal rather than God. Elijah, after his famous contest with the priests of Baal that led to his putting many of them to death, was himself being pursued. In a moment of discouragement, Elijah called out to God, complaining that he was the only faithful Israelite left and that he was being threatened with death. God responded to Elijah that he was not alone, that there were seven thousand who had remained faithful. Paul's point in alluding to this story is that, while he can hold himself up as an example of a Jew who responded with faith to the gospel, there were many more who had done so as well. These are the faithful remnant, sustained by God's grace and God's grace alone. Indeed, the apostle knew full well the power of God's grace, because at the moment he was encountered and called by the risen Lord, he had been persecuting the church (which at that time had consisted primarily of Jewish followers of the gospel).

Paul's references to the **"hardening" of Israel** (9:18; 11:7, 25) echo passages from Exodus about the hardening of Pharaoh's heart at the time of the exodus (e.g., Exod 10:27). This biblical concept doesn't mean that God steamrolls human free will, but it does minimize human culpability and emphasizes the primacy of God's ultimate will and plan.

Before transitioning to a consideration of what the future holds, Paul once again reviews the present situation: The righteousness that the majority of Israel sought but did not find, the "elect," or the remnant, had attained. He then cites an amalgam of texts from Deuteronomy, Isaiah, and Psalms that describes those who sought but did not find: Their eyes and ears have been dulled (see also 2 Cor 3:14). The apostle's citation of Scripture is not intended to suggest that God is capricious; rather, nothing happens without God's knowing and willing it. Moreover, as we will see in the next verse, the hardening of some hearts has led to the bearing of much fruit among the Gentiles.

11:11-24 The Gentiles' Salvation

In 11:11, Paul makes an important distinction. Unbelieving Israel has not fallen (suggesting a permanent situation) but has merely stumbled (suggesting the possibility of getting up again). Israel's rejection of the revelation of God's righteousness through Jesus has led to "enrichment for the Gentiles." If such is the case now (with a diminished number of Jewish believers), how much more will be the case when there will be more than a remnant? Indeed, the increase of Jewish believers will be tantamount to their coming to "life from the dead" and will lead to greater reconciliation in the world (recall 5:10-11). It is important to note here that the apostle's language of "rejection"

God's Irrevocable Call

[25]I do not want you to be unaware of this mystery, brothers, so that you will not become wise [in] your own estimation: a hardening has come upon Israel in part, until the full number of the Gentiles comes in, [26]and thus all Israel will be saved, as it is written:

"The deliverer will come out of Zion,
he will turn away godlessness from Jacob;
[27]and this is my covenant with them
when I take away their sins."

[28]In respect to the gospel, they are enemies on your account; but in respect to election, they are beloved because of the patriarchs. [29]For the gifts and the call of God are irrevocable.

continue

***Nostra Aetate* and Romans 11**

Nostra Aetate, Vatican II's Declaration on the Relation of the Church to Non-Christian Religions, relies heavily on Romans 11 in its reflection on Jewish-Christian relations:

> Sounding the depths of the mystery which is the church, this sacred council remembers the spiritual ties which link the people of the new covenant to the stock of Abraham. . . .
>
> [T]he church cannot forget that it received the revelation of the Old Testament by way of that people with whom God in his inexpressible mercy established the ancient covenant. Nor can it forget that it draws nourishment from that good olive tree onto which the wild olive branches of the Gentiles have been grafted (see Rom 11:17-24). The church believes that Christ who is our peace has through his cross reconciled Jews and Gentiles and made them one in himself (see Eph 2:14-16).
>
> Likewise, the church keeps ever before its mind the words of the apostle Paul about his kin: "they are Israelites, and it is for them to be sons and daughters, to them belong the glory, the covenants, the giving of the law, the worship, and the promises; to them belong the patriarchs, and of their race according to the flesh, is the Christ" (Rom 9:4-5). . . .
>
> Even so, the apostle Paul maintains that the Jews remain very dear to God, for the sake of the patriarchs, since God does not take back the gifts he bestowed or the choice he made (see Rom 11:28-29). Together with the prophets and that same apostle, the church awaits the day, known to God alone, when all peoples will call on God with one voice and "serve him shoulder to shoulder" (Zeph 3:9; see Isa 66:23; Ps 65:4; Rom 11:11-32). (*NA* 4)

> ***Triumph of God's Mercy***
>
> [30]Just as you once disobeyed God but have now received mercy because of their disobedience, [31]so they have now disobeyed in order that, by virtue of the mercy shown to you, they too may [now] receive mercy. [32]For God delivered all to disobedience, that he might have mercy upon all.
>
> [33]Oh, the depth of the riches and wisdom and knowledge of God! How inscrutable are his judgments and how unsearchable his ways!
>
> [34]"For who has known the mind of the Lord
> or who has been his counselor?"
> [35]"Or who has given him anything
> that he may be repaid?"
>
> [36]For from him and through him and for him are all things. To him be glory forever. Amen.

(11:15) does not point to God's rejection of Israel; rather, it is to the rejection of the gospel message by some Jews.

In his role as apostle to the Gentiles (see Gal 1:16; 2:7), Paul now directly addresses the Gentile members of the church in Rome. Reading between the lines, it seems that some of them considered themselves to be superior to the church's Jewish members. As we discussed in the Introduction, some leading Jewish members of the community had been exiled by the emperor Claudius, and in their absence, some Gentile members likely filled the resulting vacuum of leadership in the community. In this context, Paul felt the need to let the Gentiles know their place in God's plans. What follows is a call to humility and gratitude.

Paul's mention of his strategy of making his fellow Jews jealous of what was happening among the Gentiles merits reflection. His point was not to manipulate his fellow Jews but to evoke excitement about the Jew and Gentile family of faith so that others would want to join. We can ask ourselves whether our faith communities today worship and live in such a way that they attract others to join us.

While the apostle sought to attract more Jewish believers to the Jew and Gentile family of faith, he also makes clear the priority of Israel's role in God's plan of salvation. Here Paul offers his famous teaching on the olive tree (11:16-24). The tree is a metaphor for God's people, whose holiness can be attributed to its root. What is the root of this great tree? At one level, it is Abraham and his faithful response to God's promises of a family of faith that includes both Jews and Gentiles. At a deeper level, it is Christ himself. The apostle's example of an olive tree is quite apt. Just as its oily sap is the lifeblood of the tree, so through Christ (the "anointed one") is the family of faith made holy. It is surely no accident that the sacraments of baptism, confirmation, and priestly ordination involve the anointing of recipients with oil (called, appropriately, sacred chrism).

Paul's example of grafting branches onto the olive tree is an adaptation of the practice of grafting cultivated branches onto a wild tree to redirect its energies to produce more fruit. In this case, it is the wild branches that are being grafted onto a cultivated tree. The "natural branches" represent the Jews, while the Gentiles are a "wild olive shoot." This is a reminder to the Gentiles of the prominent place of Israel in God's plan of salvation, and a summons to the Gentile believers to humility. The natural branches that are on the tree are the Jews who have accepted with faith the gospel proclamation; the branches that have been broken off are Jews who have not. But just as wild branches can be grafted onto the tree, so too can the branches that have broken off. In fact, their being grafted on is more natural, because they belong "by nature" to the tree. Paul is clear that the Gentiles have not replaced the Jews in God's plan or God's church. Both constitute membership in the family of faith.

11:25-29 God's Irrevocable Call

Paul brings his retelling of the story of Israel to a climax by revealing what he calls a "mystery." Once again, he acknowledges that a "hardening" has affected some Jews regarding the gospel proclamation, leading to outreach to the Gentiles until their "full number" are joined to the family of faith. (That number is not clear, though it seems that Paul hoped that all people would have a chance to hear the gospel proclamation.) When this number is reached—and here the apostle makes a stunning, hope-filled declaration—"all Israel will be saved." What precisely Paul meant by "all Israel" and how they would be saved has been the source of much theological debate. My opinion is that, for Paul, "all Israel" referred, in addition to the remnant, to those Jews who would come to believe in the gospel proclamation. They would do so, as happened to Paul himself, through an encounter with the glorious, risen Lord, likely at the Parousia, the second coming of Christ. Of course, it was Paul's hope that every one of his Jewish brothers and sisters would come to believe in the gospel.

The apostle's concern was always more about the community of faith than individual believers (hence "all Israel"). He bolsters his claim with an amalgamation of Scripture texts from Isaiah, Jeremiah, and Psalms that brings together the themes of a deliverer from Zion (once again, a reference to Jesus, from the heavenly Jerusalem) and God's covenant, a covenant that includes the forgiveness of sins.

Continuing his address to the Gentiles, Paul again acknowledges that many Jews had not accepted the gospel proclamation. When he calls them "enemies," it is important to understand that he means their opposition to the gospel; they are *not* God's enemies. In fact, Paul goes on to remind the Gentiles that Israel—all Jews—are "beloved" by God because of God's "election" of the patriarchs. The apostle then offers a momentous statement, one that reverberates to this day: *God's gifts to and call of Israel are "irrevocable."* In divine righteousness and love, God has never revoked, nor will God ever revoke, the gifts (see, e.g., 9:4-5) and the merciful election of Israel.

Importantly, this Pauline statement (11:29) was cited with approval at Vatican II in *Nostra Aetate*, the document that clarified the Catholic Church's relations with other religions. By recognizing Judaism's divinely bestowed status, *Nostra Aetate* has helped to heal relations between Catholics and Jews. Here is a case where the apostle's words provide us with the basis for understanding, in a life-giving way, that both the church and Judaism are blessed by God.

11:30-36 Triumph of God's Mercy

Paul concludes his lengthy defense of God's righteousness by highlighting God's mercy. Both Jews and Gentiles have been disobedient in their own ways toward God, and both have received divine mercy. God's righteousness and love are such that divine justice is a saving justice, marked by mercy.

This reality leads the apostle to offer praise to God. The citation of Isaiah 40:13 in verse 34 functions to stress the great difference between the Creator and creatures. God's creatures are to respond, as the closing chapters of Romans will reveal, with obedience to God and God's ways, following the example of the faithful Jesus.

EXPLORING LESSON FOUR

1. What major difficulty or question is Paul addressing in Romans 9–11?

2. Paul felt a deep loyalty to his Jewish brothers and sisters who had not accepted Jesus as the Messiah (9:1-5). Have you ever been in a situation where you felt a strong loyalty to someone even though you may not have agreed with them about something important? Does this help you understand how conflicted Paul felt?

3. Paul's review of Israelite history in 9:6-24 emphasizes God's freedom from human conventions and expectations. When have you seen God working in your life in an unexpected way that turned out to be a blessing?

4. Why was the cross of Jesus a "stumbling block" or "scandal" for the Jewish people in terms of believing Jesus was the Messiah (9:32-33; see Deut 21:22-23)?

5. According to the commentary, what does Paul mean when he says that "Christ is the end of the law" (10:4)?

6. As you read 11:1-10, refresh yourself on the transformation of Paul from persecutor of the church to apostle by reading Acts 7:54-60; 8:1-3; and 9:1-19. (In these texts Paul is referred to by his Jewish name, Saul.) How do you think this personal experience helped Paul to be empathetic toward his Jewish brothers and sisters who did not believe Jesus was the Messiah?

7. How would you summarize Paul's essential message to Gentile believers in 11:13-24?

8. In what ways do you see the Jewish roots of Christianity continuing to nurture the church (see Rom 4:16; 15:4; Matt 13:52; Mark 14:12-24)?

9. a) What is Paul's certainty regarding Israel and its relationship with God (11:25-29)?

   b) How has the church highlighted this truth in the modern era, and how has this emphasis helped to heal relations between Catholics and Jews?

10. Paul closes this section with a powerful affirmation of God's mercy on all people (11:30-36). How have you experienced God's mercy—either as an individual or as a member of your church or nation? How are you being called to extend this mercy into the world?

CLOSING PRAYER

[T]he gifts and the call of God are irrevocable.
(Rom 11:29)

Loving and merciful God, we thank you for your covenant fidelity to the Jewish people and to us. Help us to recognize, appreciate, and cherish the Jewish heritage that underlies our faith. Today we pray for all of our Jewish brothers and sisters, as well as . . .

LESSON FIVE

Romans 12:1–15:13

Begin your personal study and group discussion with a simple and sincere prayer such as:

Prayer

Loving God, send your Spirit upon us as we study the writings of your apostle Paul. Open our ears, our minds, and especially our hearts. Deepen your love within us, and transform us to embody and proclaim the good news you have revealed in your son Jesus Christ.

Read the Bible text of Romans 12:1–15:13, found in the outside columns of pages 78–87, highlighting what stands out to you.

Read the accompanying commentary to add to your understanding.

Respond to the questions on pages 88–90, Exploring Lesson Five.

The Closing Prayer on page 91 is for your personal use and may be used at the end of group discussion.

VI: The Duties of Christians

CHAPTER 12

Sacrifice of Body and Mind

1I urge you therefore, brothers, by the mercies of God, to offer your bodies as a living sacrifice, holy and pleasing to God, your spiritual worship. 2Do not conform yourselves to this age but be transformed by the renewal of your mind, that you may discern what is the will of God, what is good and pleasing and perfect.

continue

THE DUTIES OF CHRISTIANS

Romans 12:1–15:13

Having set forth how God's righteousness has been revealed through Jesus' faithfulness-unto-death and through the sending of the Spirit, and having defended God's righteousness with regard to Israel, Paul now turns to offering exhortations and encouragement to the members of the house churches in Rome. He calls them to embody God's righteousness—self-giving love after the manner of Jesus—in all aspects of their lives.

12:1-2 Sacrifice of Body and Mind

Paul begins by appealing to the Roman Christians "by the mercies of God." Recall that he just finished his prior exposition by highlighting how God has been merciful to all, to both Jews and Gentiles. God's mercy is the basis of their relationship with the divine and the motivation for how they should conduct themselves.

These two verses lay the foundation for all that follows in the letter. They thus require our close attention. Paul calls Christian life "a living sacrifice" to God. In his time, sacrifices to the gods (including to God in the Jerusalem temple) usually culminated in the death of an animal, so the idea of a living sacrifice would have been striking. The apostle calls for a way of living that involves the *whole* person—body and mind—in service of God. The practice of making a morning "offering" in prayer to God is a good way to instill within ourselves this way of looking at our service to God. Such prayers often mention offering to God all our prayers, works, and sufferings, and all that we think, do, and say.

It is significant to point out that the Greek phrase translated as "spiritual worship" is *logikos latreia*, which suggests a cognitive element. Sure enough, Paul then exhorts: "[B]e transformed by the renewal of your mind." There is much to be gleaned from this phrasing. First, his use of the passive voice suggests that *God* (through the Spirit) is the active agent. The use of the passive voice is a way that Jews, like Paul, showed reverence for the divine name, which was never to be casually pronounced. The verb "transformed" translates a Greek word from which we get "metamorphosis," thereby suggesting a major change and maturation. What this change entails is an authentic "renewal of the mind."

The apostle's meaning can be further understood by recalling what he writes in 2 Corinthians 3:18: By contemplating Christ and his ways, we are "being transformed into the same image [i.e., into the image of Christ, who is the image of God *par excellence*; see 2 Cor 4:4] from glory to glory, as from the Lord who is the Spirit." Paul is calling on the members of the community to be alert and open to empowerment by the Spirit to become more Christlike. They do so by allowing the Spirit, in their prayer, to intercede for and enable them to take on "the mind of Christ" (1 Cor 2:16)—that is, Christ's way of seeing and valuing persons and situations. As we saw in 8:26-27, the Spirit does this for us "according to God's will." To discern (another fruit of prayer) how to live in accord with God's will, after the manner of Jesus' obedience, is to live in the new creation by doing "what is good and pleasing and perfect," and not conforming to the ways of the world.

Another word about the new creation: It is realized more and more when we grow into our potential of being transformed into the image of God as manifested by Jesus. The Greek word usually translated as "image" is *eikōn*, from which we get the word "icon." Just as a good icon draws our attention to look through it as if it were a window to reflect on the image being portrayed (e.g., Jesus, one of the saints, or a scene from the Gospels), so people should be able to look at us and learn something about God's love and goodness in us.

Many Parts in One Body

3For by the grace given to me I tell everyone among you not to think of himself more highly than one ought to think, but to think soberly, each according to the measure of faith that God has apportioned. 4For as in one body we have many parts, and all the parts do not have the same function, 5so we, though many, are one body in Christ and individually parts of one another. 6Since we have gifts that differ according to the grace given to us, let us exercise them: if prophecy, in proportion to the faith; 7if ministry, in ministering; if one is a teacher, in teaching; 8if one exhorts, in exhortation; if one contributes, in generosity; if one is over others, with diligence; if one does acts of mercy, with cheerfulness.

Mutual Love

9Let love be sincere; hate what is evil, hold on to what is good; 10love one another with mutual affection; anticipate one another in showing honor. 11Do not grow slack in zeal, be fervent in spirit, serve the Lord. 12Rejoice in hope, endure in affliction, persevere in prayer. 13Contribute to the needs of the holy ones, exercise hospitality.

continue

12:3-8 Many Parts in One Body

In 12:3-8, Paul reminds the Roman Christians, via a metaphor of the body, of their communal identity. As a community of faith, they constitute "one body in Christ." Christian life is enacted in the context of community (recall the earlier comments about covenant), and this involves using God-given gifts for building up the community of faith. This reality calls for humility, because God is the giver of gifts; they are not self-generated. Moreover, we are all interdependent; none of us can afford to be a lone ranger. We are also called to sensitivity to the needs of others, to generosity of spirit, and to commitment to the common good. A helpful litmus test of our spiritual growth in these connections is to ask: Can we truly rejoice in the gifts and successes of others? Or do we find ourselves overly focusing on ourselves? Another important feature is that, when Paul refers to local communities as the "body of Christ" or "Christ's body," (see, e.g., 1 Cor 12:27), he intends more than a metaphor. As "Christ's body," local communities are to *incarnate* Christ's presence and enact his ministry for those around them. They are thus a special means by which Jesus is present in the world today.

12:9-21 Mutual Love

To incarnate Christ's presence is to grow in the ways of love, and Paul offers a good deal of practical advice. Genuine (or sincere) love is proactive, looking for ways to show kindness to others, anticipating their needs, showing empathy, and offering hospitality to them (a particularly apt exhortation in a context of

[14]Bless those who persecute [you], bless and do not curse them. [15]Rejoice with those who rejoice, weep with those who weep. [16]Have the same regard for one another; do not be haughty but associate with the lowly; do not be wise in your own estimation.[17]Do not repay anyone evil for evil; be concerned for what is noble in the sight of all. [18]If possible, on your part, live at peace with all. [19]Beloved, do not look for revenge but leave room for the wrath; for it is written, "Vengeance is mine, I will repay, says the Lord." [20]Rather, "if your enemy is hungry, feed him; if he is thirsty, give him something to drink; for by so doing you will heap burning coals upon his head." [21]Do not be conquered by evil but conquer evil with good.

CHAPTER 13

Obedience to Authority

[1]Let every person be subordinate to the higher authorities, for there is no authority except from God, and those that exist have been established by God. [2]Therefore, whoever resists authority opposes what God has appointed, and those who oppose it will bring judgment upon themselves. [3]For rulers are not a cause of fear to good conduct, but to evil. Do you wish to have no fear of authority? Then do what is good and you will receive approval from it, [4]for it is a servant of God for your good. But if you do evil, be afraid, for it does not bear the sword without purpose; it is the servant of God to inflict wrath on the evildoer. [5]Therefore, it is necessary to be subject not only

continue

house churches that were likely divided along ethnic lines). Such love is not divisive but spurns the desire for revenge and takes the initiative to forgive, and to seek reconciliation and the healing of relationships.

Paul then transitions to relationships beyond the community. When he calls for nonretaliation, and for blessing those who show animosity toward and persecute members of the community, he echoes Jesus' most difficult teachings, including love of one's enemies (see Matt 5:38-48). Jesus' commands in this regard (including the commitment to nonviolence) are difficult, to say the least. They also testify to the power of love in the family of faith. Recall the rationale Jesus offers for such expansive and radical love: This is how God's children are to grow in the way of perfection, manifesting the trait that particularly marks God's family (see Matt 5:48).

Paul's comment that, in treating one's enemies with kindness, one is, in effect, heaping coals upon their heads has struck some as vindictive. But we should read verses 19-20 within Paul's wider context of nonretaliation and peaceful living. It is likely that Paul's ultimate point is not the humiliation of one's enemies but hope for motivation toward their own transformation in Christ.

13:1-7 Obedience to Authority

Continuing his transition from intracommunity relations, the apostle now turns to address the question of how Christians should behave vis-à-vis governing authorities. This passage may have exerted as much, if not more, influence over time than any other passage in Romans. Oppressive regimes have appealed to it to demand loyalty and obedience from their Christian subjects. Paul would be horrified by such use of his teaching. To be sure, he held a benevolent view of government. He believed that God desired good social order, and that governing authorities ruled by divine will. Thus, as citizens, it is important for believers to contribute to the good order of society—including payment of their taxes.

But notice how Paul describes authorities. They are God's "servant[s]" and thus are answerable to God for their ways of governing. To appeal to Paul's letter for blind obedience to any authority is wrong. In fact, the apostle's preaching of Jesus as Messiah (i.e., King) was a threat to imperial power, because the gospel challenged many aspects of Roman life and society (see, e.g., Acts 16:20). It is no accident that Paul was put to death by Roman authorities. Obedience and cooperation with governing authorities presume a just social order. Our ultimate loyalty is always, and in every case, owed first and foremost to God and God's ways.

13:8-10 Love Fulfills the Law

Paul's point in this section is simple: What is owed to others is love. Love, in the sense of *agapē*, is the commitment to act always for the good of the other. Hence, there is no room for selfishness in *agapē*; rather, it presumes a stance of respectful, attentive openness to learning and hearing what others truly need to be built up and cared for. As we saw in 8:4, the Spirit empowers us to fulfill the "righteous decree" or the "just requirement" (NRSV) of the law, which is, as Jesus taught, to love one's neighbor as oneself (Matt 22:37-39; see Lev 19:18). Here, Paul echoes the teaching of Jesus: To fulfill the law of love of God and neighbor is "the fulfillment of the law."

because of the wrath but also because of con-
science. [6]This is why you also pay taxes, for the
authorities are ministers of God, devoting them-
selves to this very thing. [7]Pay to all their dues,
taxes to whom taxes are due, toll to whom toll is
due, respect to whom respect is due, honor to
whom honor is due.

Love Fulfills the Law

[8]Owe nothing to anyone, except to love one
another; for the one who loves another has ful-
filled the law. [9]The commandments, "You shall
not commit adultery; you shall not kill; you shall
not steal; you shall not covet," and whatever other
commandment there may be, are summed up in
this saying, [namely] "You shall love your neigh-
bor as yourself." [10]Love does no evil to the neigh-
bor; hence, love is the fulfillment of the law.

continue

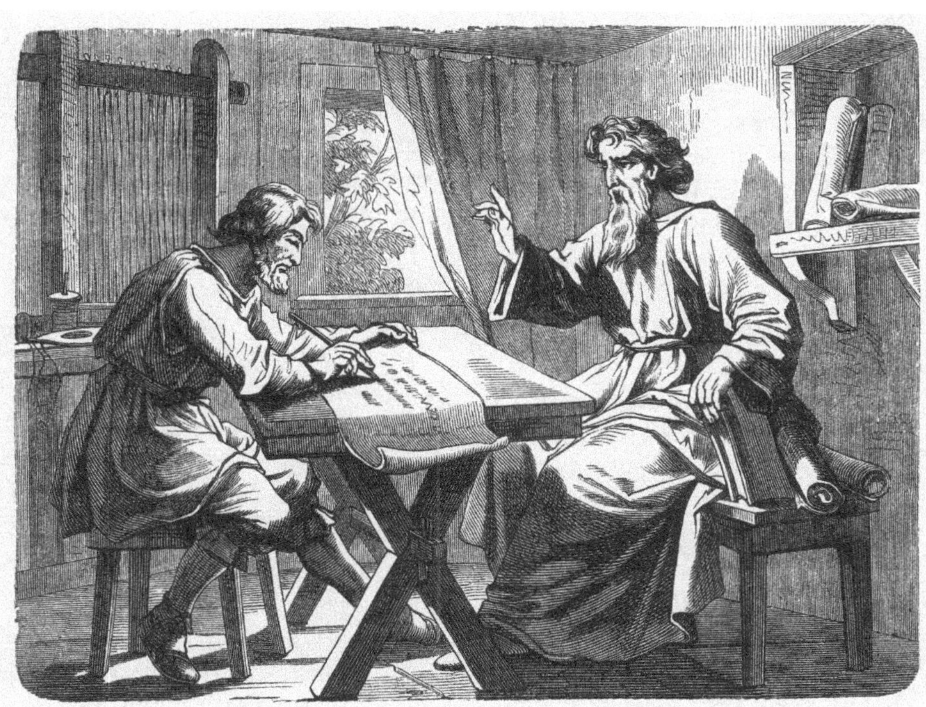

Paul dictating his letter to the Roman Christians to Tertius (16:22). Woodcut after a drawing by Julius Schnorr von Carolsfeld.

Awareness of the End of Time

11And do this because you know the time; it is
the hour now for you to awake from sleep. For
our salvation is nearer now than when we first
believed; 12the night is advanced, the day is at
hand. Let us then throw off the works of darkness
[and] put on the armor of light; 13let us conduct
ourselves properly as in the day, not in orgies and
drunkenness, not in promiscuity and licentious-
ness, not in rivalry and jealousy. 14But put on the
Lord Jesus Christ, and make no provision for the
desires of the flesh.

CHAPTER 14

To Live and Die for Christ

1Welcome anyone who is weak in faith, but
not for disputes over opinions. 2One person be-
lieves that one may eat anything, while the weak
person eats only vegetables. 3The one who eats
must not despise the one who abstains, and the
one who abstains must not pass judgment on the
one who eats; for God has welcomed him. 4Who
are you to pass judgment on someone else's ser-
vant? Before his own master he stands or falls.
And he will be upheld, for the Lord is able to
make him stand. 5[For] one person considers one
day more important than another, while another
person considers all days alike. Let everyone be
fully persuaded in his own mind. 6Whoever ob-
serves the day, observes it for the Lord. Also who-
ever eats, eats for the Lord, since he gives thanks
to God; while whoever abstains, abstains for the
Lord and gives thanks to God. 7None of us lives
for oneself, and no one dies for oneself. 8For if we
live, we live for the Lord, and if we die, we die for
the Lord; so then, whether we live or die, we are

continue

13:11-14 Awareness of the End of Time

One piece of information that we always like to know at any moment in our lives is what time it is. That is because our lives tend to be tightly scheduled. Paul reminds the Roman community about what time it is and how they should respond. However, he employs a special word for "time" that will be helpful for us to understand. Greek has two words for "time." One is *chronos* (from which we get the word "chronology"), which is time as we usually think of it: minute by minute, hour by hour, day by day, etc. The other is *kairos*, the word the apostle uses here, which means "opportune time."

Paul calls the Roman believers to recognize that, through Christ and the gift of the Spirit, they are called to be people of light and day. Using the imagery of changing from night clothes to what is appropriate to wear for the day, he calls them to cast off "works of darkness." We tend to cover up and hide the things we are ashamed of. A good antidote is to be transparent to others in our words and actions, letting God's light shine through us (see Matt 5:14-16). Notice that Paul mentions two types of "clothing" to put on. One is the "armor of light," which suggests that Christian living can be a challenge in the face of worldly pressures and requires God's help and protection (see, e.g., Eph 6:10-17). Second, he exhorts his audience to "put on the Lord Jesus Christ." In baptism we were clothed with Christ (Gal 3:27), and through the Spirit's empowerment we can "put on" Jesus' distinguishing qualities: compassion, meekness, kindness, patience, forbearance (see Col 3:12-13). In doing so, we live in the Spirit and not in the flesh.

The text of Romans 13:13-14 was key to the **conversion of St. Augustine**. One day Augustine, who was full of doubt and turmoil, heard a voice telling him to "take and read." He rushed to his home where he had a copy of Paul's Letter to the Romans. He opened it, and his eyes fell on these verses. After reading them, Augustine felt certainty wash over him and a light in his heart. He gave his life to God and never looked back. Augustine returned to the text of Romans often throughout his life as a believer, a bishop, and a theologian.

14:1-12 To Live and Die for Christ

In this passage, Paul does what he does in most of his letters: He addresses questions and concerns that have been brought to his attention. One might ask: How would Paul have known what was going on in Rome, since he had yet to visit the house churches there? As we will see when we arrive at Romans 16, Paul already knew a number of people in the community. These individuals may have been the source of his information and may have asked him to respond.

One issue revolved around what were appropriate foods to eat. Some of the Jewish members likely preferred to eat only kosher food (e.g., vegetables). Another issue was the celebration of Jewish feast days and, possibly, observance of the Sabbath. These were not trivial issues, to say the least. It is important for communities of faith to be able to enjoy table fellowship (i.e., to be "companions" in the literal sense of sharing bread with one another) and to worship together in harmony. It appears that two different factions arose. One faction, what we today might call the "traditionalists," was quick to condemn those it regarded as being overly lax about such things. The other, what might be named the "progressives," looked down condescendingly on those it viewed as stuck in old ways. To make matters worse, the more conservative members were dubbed as "weak" by the other group, who regarded themselves as "strong." (These groups did not divide strictly along ethnic lines, as we will see.) Does all this sound eerily familiar? The apostle's admonitions are as timely now as ever.

Paul calls for an end to passing judgment and looking down on fellow community members. He reminds everyone that God has called each and every member and has welcomed them into the community of faith. So, too, are they now to welcome one another. Each member is accountable to God as their Lord and Master. Who are they to take God's role in judging (see the discussion of 2:1-11 above)? The apostle instructs the community that quarreling over such things has no place in the family of faith. What is more important than being "right" in debates about such matters is to love after the manner of Jesus. It is to him we belong, in life and death. As long as members are acting in good faith—that is, eating and celebrating (or not) by giving thanks and praise to God—they should be respected. Paul is clear that there is room for diversity in the family of faith. In fact, the image of the community as the Body of Christ (see commentary on 12:3-8) has illustrated this same point. Believers are to embody and show forth a reconciled community that bears authentic witness to the gospel that proclaims the reconciling effects of Jesus' death (see 5:10-11).

the Lord's. 9For this is why Christ died and came
to life, that he might be Lord of both the dead
and the living. 10Why then do you judge your
brother? Or you, why do you look down on your
brother? For we shall all stand before the judg-
ment seat of God; 11for it is written:

> "As I live, says the Lord, every knee shall
> bend before me,
> and every tongue shall give praise to God."

12So [then] each of us shall give an account of him-
self [to God].

Consideration for the Weak Conscience

13Then let us no longer judge one another, but
rather resolve never to put a stumbling block or
hindrance in the way of a brother. 14I know and
am convinced in the Lord Jesus that nothing is
unclean in itself; still, it is unclean for someone
who thinks it unclean. 15If your brother is being
hurt by what you eat, your conduct is no longer

continue

14:13-23 Consideration for the Weak Conscience

Paul now offers an example of the type of unifying, reconciling behavior the gospel demands. It is important for us to appreciate that many meats, other foods, and even wine (think

in accord with love. Do not because of your food
destroy him for whom Christ died. [16]So do not
let your good be reviled. [17]For the kingdom of
God is not a matter of food and drink, but of
righteousness, peace, and joy in the holy Spirit;
[18]whoever serves Christ in this way is pleasing to
God and approved by others. [19]Let us then pursue
what leads to peace and to building up one an-
other. [20]For the sake of food, do not destroy the
work of God. Everything is indeed clean, but it is
wrong for anyone to become a stumbling block
by eating; [21]it is good not to eat meat or drink
wine or do anything that causes your brother to
stumble. [22]Keep the faith [that] you have to your-
self in the presence of God; blessed is the one who
does not condemn himself for what he approves.
[23]But whoever has doubts is condemned if he eats,
because this is not from faith; for whatever is not
from faith is sin.

continue

libations to the gods) in his time were involved in some type of pagan sacrifice or prayer to idols—whether at public celebrations, temple sacrifices, or dinners hosted by a pagan colleague or friend. Thus, the question arose about the propriety of eating and drinking them. The "strong," like Paul, reasoned that in Christ "nothing is unclean in itself" (see, e.g., Mark 7:19). But there were members whose consciences were sensitive and for whom some foods and drink were not to be consumed because of their involvement in idol worship. (Indeed, the issues were very complex, as the lengthy treatment in 1 Cor 9–11 reveals.)

The apostle asserted the primacy of conscience and the necessity of acting according to it. If someone thought, in good conscience, that it was wrong to partake of such food and drink, then they should refrain from consuming them. Moreover, Paul insisted that the "strong" respect those who were weaker in conscience. To eat and drink disputed items in their presence could scandalize them and lead them to sin. He called the "strong" to sacrifice what they thought was their "right" for the sake of a sensitive community member, and to recall the sacrifice Christ made for all. He exhorted members of the community to regard one another not only as brothers and sisters but also as brothers or sisters "for whom Christ died." This is an expression of authentic freedom: to sacrifice voluntarily, out of love, for the sake of a fellow community member, for their support and building up.

Prayer Starter: Is there someone in your life who you find difficult to love? Paul's reminder that Christ died for each and every person can be helpful. Imagine this person in the presence of Christ. Be reminded how much Christ loves them. Allow this imaginative exercise to lead you into prayer. It just might transform your relationship.

Unfortunately, in today's cultural context, freedom is rarely understood in this way. Here is where Christians have something of great value to offer to others. The same was true in the apostle's time. These values were in stark contrast to the Roman *pater familias* way of being family that was marked by hierarchy and power, centered on the head of the family. The family of faith thereby bore witness to an alternative way of being together, which some in Roman society regarded as a threat to their way of being. Paul's call for living in authentic freedom, with sensitivity to others and a willingness to make personal sacrifices, is thus also a call to courage.

In 14:17, Paul refers explicitly to "the kingdom of God" for the first and only time in Romans (although, as we saw with the language of "reigning" in 5:17-21, the "kingdom" has been in the background of his presentation). Notice how Paul describes it. Negatively put, it is not about food and drink; even more, it is not about insisting on one's preferences and conveniences. Positively expressed, it is about "righteousness, peace, and joy in the holy

Spirit." Paul's wording is hardly accidental. "Righteousness" refers to God's covenant faithfulness revealed through Jesus' self-giving love and the outpouring of the Holy Spirit (as alluded to at the end of the list). "Peace" points to the result of being reconciled with God and with one another. "Joy" is a "fruit" of the Spirit poured into our hearts (see Gal 5:22).

When the apostle goes on to comment that "whatever is not from faith is sin" (14:23), he is emphasizing the preeminence of a faith-informed conscience for life in the new creation.

Vatican II emphasized the importance of **conscience**, describing it as a way that human beings encounter God: "Their conscience is people's most secret core, and their sanctuary. There they are alone with God whose voice echoes in their depths." Following one's conscience is essential: "For they have in their hearts a law inscribed by God. Their dignity rests in observing this law, and by it they will be judged" (*Gaudium et Spes* 16).

CHAPTER 15

Patience and Self-Denial

1We who are strong ought to put up with the
failings of the weak and not to please ourselves;
2let each of us please our neighbor for the good,
for building up. 3For Christ did not please him-
self; but, as it is written, "The insults of those who
insult you fall upon me." 4For whatever was writ-
ten previously was written for our instruction,
that by endurance and by the encouragement of
the scriptures we might have hope. 5May the God
of endurance and encouragement grant you to
think in harmony with one another, in keeping
with Christ Jesus, 6that with one accord you may
with one voice glorify the God and Father of our
Lord Jesus Christ.

continue

15:1-6 Patience and Self-Denial

Aligning himself with the "strong," Paul now exhorts the community in Rome to bear with the "weaknesses" (not "failings," as the NABRE translation wrongly sets forth) of the "weak." This is more than a call for tolerance, though it is certainly that. It is also a call to bear one another's burdens (see Gal 6:2) and to build others up. This is what the word "edify" means, a word that appears frequently in the apostle's exhortations. This may lead us to consider the following questions for a daily examination of conscience: Did my words and actions today build up and encourage others? Or did they tear them down in discouragement or shame? Rather than strive always to please oneself, members of the reconciled community of faith are to be committed to seeking what is best for their "neighbor." Paul's use of the latter term recalls his teaching about love of neighbor as fulfillment of the law (see 13:9). In this case, such love surely includes doing what one can to build up, to help the so-called "weak" members to mature in their faith.

Paul then holds up the example of Jesus, who did not seek his own good but sought that of others. In quoting Psalm 69 (a psalm about a righteous sufferer who was vindicated by God for his faithfulness) in 15:3, the apostle had Jesus in mind. He then goes on to make a crucially important statement about Scripture and its ongoing significance. Psalm 69, written long ago but now understood christologically (i.e., as pertaining to Jesus), was "written for our instruction." Jesus' way of offering his life for others serves as an example that is always relevant.

We should remind ourselves that Paul's Letter to the Romans, written some 2,000 years ago, in a particular context, was also written for *our* instruction today, as God's word to us. This living word of God gives us the wherewithal to persevere in the way of living set forth by Jesus. By having the mind and love of Jesus (see Phil 2:2-11), the community of faith incarnates the harmony and reconciliation made possible by the Spirit. In doing so, it

God's Fidelity and Mercy

[7]Welcome one another, then, as Christ welcomed you, for the glory of God. [8]For I say that Christ became a minister of the circumcised to show God's truthfulness, to confirm the promises to the patriarchs, [9]but so that the Gentiles might glorify God for his mercy. As it is written:

"Therefore, I will praise you among the
Gentiles
and sing praises to your name."

[10]And again it says:

"Rejoice, O Gentiles, with his people."

[11]And again:

"Praise the Lord, all you Gentiles,
and let all the peoples praise him."

[12]And again Isaiah says:

"The root of Jesse shall come,
raised up to rule the Gentiles;
in him shall the Gentiles hope."

[13]May the God of hope fill you with all joy and peace in believing, so that you may abound in hope by the power of the holy Spirit.

gives proper glory and praise to God and to Jesus as Lord. We can let our conviction of this ongoing power of God's word motivate our continued commitment to study and prayerfully reflect on Scripture throughout our lives—especially as it is offered to us from the "table of the Word" in eucharistic celebrations.

The apostle's brief descriptions of God are easy to pass over quickly. But they are worth our reflection. In 2:4, Paul highlighted God's "kindness, forbearance, and patience," all of which are aligned with divine mercy. The present depiction of God's "endurance and encouragement" alludes to God's covenant faithfulness and to the divine impetus to "put into the heart," the literal meaning of the word "encourage." Of course, God has put into our hearts the Spirit of love (5:5). Understanding these aspects of God is vitally important for us who are created in the divine likeness. While it is beyond our capacity to bestow the Spirit on others, we can grow in faithfulness, kindness, forbearance, and patience and be people who encourage one another day by day (see 2 Cor 1:3-7).

15:7-13 God's Fidelity and Mercy

Paul concludes this section on a liturgical note. He exhorts the faithful in Rome to "[w]elcome one another" as fellow brothers and sisters in the family of faith. He gives the example of Jesus' welcome, his way of inclusive love, for their mutual welcoming as a reconciled community of faith. Notice how Paul refers to Christ here: as a "minister" (*diakonos*, meaning "one who serves") to the "circumcised." That Jesus is described as a "minister" evokes his self-description as one who "did not come to be served but to serve and to give his life as a ransom for many" (see Mark 10:45). The reference to Jesus' ministry among the circumcised points to the fact that his mission was first and foremost among his own people, "the house of Israel" (see, e.g., Matt 10:6). Through this mission and ministry, Jesus manifested God's "truthfulness" (covenant faithfulness) and fulfilled the divine promises to Abraham, Isaac, and Jacob (9:4-5). Jesus' ministry, though directed mostly to Jews, also reached out to Gentiles (see, e.g., Matt 8:5-13; 15:21-28). In 15:9 (where the first word should be translated "and," not "but," because the emphasis is on continuity, not contrast), the apostle begins to cite a series of biblical texts (from Deuteronomy, Psalms, and the prophet Isaiah) that prophesy that the Gentiles would join the Jews in praising God, especially when the "root of Jesse" (the Messiah) comes. Here is another intimation of Paul's vision of the Jew and Gentile family of faith.

What is particularly relevant for our purposes is the image of this family of faith coming together in worship. The church is most itself—that is, truest to its identity as the community of faith—when it gathers at liturgy to give thanks and praise to God. It is at the eucharistic liturgy that the assembly is nourished by Word and sacrament, being made holy through the gift of the Spirit.

Most appropriately, Paul ends with a prayer here, calling on "the God of hope" (another description of God) to fill the community with the gifts of joy and peace. Such gifts are a consequence of our being formed as the reconciled Body of Christ. We will then "abound in hope by the power of the holy Spirit," the divine gift of love poured into our hearts (see 5:5). In a world largely devoid of hope, our witness to it ought never to be underestimated.

EXPLORING LESSON FIVE

1. How is the practice of offering ourselves to God as a "living sacrifice" different from Israel's practice of offering animal sacrifice as a form of worship (12:1; see also 6:13; Deut 12:13-14)?

2. Who do you know that you consider to be an "image" or an "icon" of Christ (12:2; 2 Cor 3:18)? How has this person avoided being conformed to "this age" and instead been transformed "by the renewal of [their] mind"?

3. What gift or gifts has the Spirit given to you for the sake of the Body of Christ (12:3-8; see also 1 Cor 12:4-11)? How do these gifts complement the gifts of others?

4. Read Paul's practical and spiritual exhortations in 12:9-18 out loud. Which of these exhortations resonates with you most at this time in your life and why?

5. a) Paul's exhortation to obey "higher authorities" could be read as encouraging blind obedience to all civil authority (13:1-7). What point does the commentary make that helps you interpret this passage?

b) What are the circumstances, if any, in which you think a Christian might have a moral obligation to refuse obedience to civil authority?

6. How does Paul's teaching on the fulfillment of the commandments compare with that of Jesus (13:8-10; see also Lev 19:18; Mark 12:28-33; Gal 5:14)?

7. Immediately after Paul's exhortation to love (13:8-10), he addresses tension within the Roman community over table fellowship and other practices. What is Paul's vision for how the community should handle such disagreements (14:1-23)?

8. How can we apply Paul's guidance about the primacy of conscience and the importance of sensitivity and love for one another to issues in our church communities today?

9. How has reading and studying the Bible instructed you, encouraged you, or given you hope (15:4)?

10. Paul concludes this section by recognizing the centrality and beauty of the church's unified worship of God (15:7-13). Reflect on your own experiences of communal worship. How are liturgical celebrations a reflection of your community's diversity and unity?

CLOSING PRAYER

Prayer

Welcome one another, then, as Christ welcomed you, for the glory of God. (Rom 15:7)

God of endurance and encouragement, bless and inspire our community of faith to be a place of mutual welcome. Help us to regard one another as brothers and sisters for whom Christ died, and to offer each person the love and support they need. Make us truly the Body of Christ. Today we pray especially for . . .

LESSON SIX

Romans 15:14–16:27

Begin your personal study and group discussion with a simple and sincere prayer such as:

Prayer

Loving God, send your Spirit upon us as we study the writings of your apostle Paul. Open our ears, our minds, and especially our hearts. Deepen your love within us, and transform us to embody and proclaim the good news you have revealed in your son Jesus Christ.

Read the Bible text of Romans 15:14–16:27, found in the outside columns of pages 94–102, highlighting what stands out to you.

Read the accompanying commentary to add to your understanding.

Respond to the questions on pages 103–105, Exploring Lesson Six.

The Closing Prayer on page 106 is for your personal use and may be used at the end of group discussion.

VII: Conclusion

Apostle to the Gentiles

[14]I myself am convinced about you, my broth-
ers, that you yourselves are full of goodness, filled
with all knowledge, and able to admonish one
another. [15]But I have written to you rather boldly
in some respects to remind you, because of the
grace given me by God [16]to be a minister of Christ
Jesus to the Gentiles in performing the priestly
service of the gospel of God, so that the offering
up of the Gentiles may be acceptable, sanctified
by the holy Spirit. [17]In Christ Jesus, then, I have
reason to boast in what pertains to God. [18]For I
will not dare to speak of anything except what
Christ has accomplished through me to lead the
Gentiles to obedience by word and deed, [19]by the
power of signs and wonders, by the power of the
Spirit [of God], so that from Jerusalem all the way
around to Illyricum I have finished preaching the
gospel of Christ. [20]Thus I aspire to proclaim the
gospel not where Christ has already been named,
so that I do not build on another's foundation,
[21]but as it is written:

"Those who have never been told of him
shall see,
and those who have never heard of him
shall understand."

continue

CONCLUSION

Romans 15:14–16:27

15:14-21 Apostle to the Gentiles

After his lengthy theological exposition (1:1–11:36) and series of exhortations to the community (12:1–15:13), Paul begins to bring the letter to its conclusion. He carefully balances his God-given apostolic authority with his recognition of the Roman Christians' maturity in faith and their agency. Such a balancing act can be a challenge. Good leadership in ministry should recognize and call forth the gifts of others and never devolve into lording one's authority over them.

The apostle then draws upon cultic imagery to offer a beautiful description of his own understanding of his apostolic call, one that is specially directed to Gentiles. He is a "minister" (Greek *leitourgos*, from which we get our word "liturgy") of Messiah Jesus. His proclamation of "the gospel of God" (see 1:1) and pastoral follow-up care are his "priestly service." And the Gentiles, who have responded favorably to his proclamation, are his "offering" to God. This priestly self-understanding (which draws on Paul's understanding of the Jewish priesthood) surely served as motivation and consolation for Paul. So too can our own priestly identity, bestowed on us in baptism through our anointing with the sacred chrism, undergird whatever ministries we engage in.

When sealed with the oil (chrism) of baptism, we are "incorporated into Christ who is anointed **priest, prophet, and king**" (*Catechism of the Catholic Church* 1241). This means that we too participate in these three offices—offering all things to God as priests, witnessing to the truth of the gospel as prophets, and serving others in imitation of Christ's humble kingship (see *CCC* 783–786).

This self-understanding also kept the apostle humble. He was doing the work of Christ, not his own projects. It is the Lord who empowered him to call forth the "obedience" of the Gentile believers. Indeed, he acknowledges that the Spirit worked "signs and wonders" through him.

Next, Paul sets forth his ministerial approach and offers a glimpse into what he has accomplished. His way of being an apostle has been to preach where the gospel has yet to be proclaimed, with all the challenges that entailed (see 2 Cor 10:15-16). In fact, his preaching has already extended from the area around Jerusalem all the way to Illyricum—a region including present-day nations such as Albania, Croatia, and Bosnia and Herzegovina. As we will see, having completed this work, the apostle sets his sights on Spain, the westernmost part of the empire. In 15:21, he quotes Isaiah again, with confidence that his ministry fulfills what is written in the Scriptures. This is a reminder that the story of Scripture is to continue in the life and ministry of the church today.

15:22-33 Paul's Plans; Need for Prayers

Recall from 1:9-15 that Paul had wanted to visit Rome for several years. We learn now that his work in the area around the Aegean Sea (i.e., in Philippi, Thessalonica, Corinth, Ephesus, and Troas—as recounted in the Acts of the Apostles) had prevented his coming to Rome. This work has been brought to completion, so he is ready to turn west toward Spain. But first he desires to stop in Rome to spend time in the community and then to be "sent on [his] way" to Spain. The verb translated as "send on" is *propempó*, used to connote the outfitting of someone for an expedition. This is the apostle's way of expressing his hope that the community in Rome will offer him assistance—financial and logistical, at the least—for his mission to Spain. Indeed, throughout Paul's ministry, he depended on the support and generosity of the churches he founded for such assistance, which he considered to be their partnership with him in the service of the gospel (see, e.g., Phil 4:10-20).

Paul's Plans; Need for Prayers

[22]That is why I have so often been prevented
from coming to you. [23]But now, since I no longer
have any opportunity in these regions and since
I have desired to come to you for many years, [24]I
hope to see you in passing as I go to Spain and to
be sent on my way there by you, after I have en-
joyed being with you for a time. [25]Now, however,
I am going to Jerusalem to minister to the holy
ones. [26]For Macedonia and Achaia have decided
to make some contribution for the poor among
the holy ones in Jerusalem; [27]they decided to do
it, and in fact they are indebted to them, for if the
Gentiles have come to share in their spiritual
blessings, they ought also to serve them in mate-
rial blessings. [28]So when I have completed this and
safely handed over this contribution to them, I
shall set out by way of you to Spain; [29]and I know
that in coming to you I shall come in the fullness
of Christ's blessing.

[30]I urge you, [brothers,] by our Lord Jesus
Christ and by the love of the Spirit, to join me in
the struggle by your prayers to God on my behalf,
[31]that I may be delivered from the disobedient in
Judea, and that my ministry for Jerusalem may be
acceptable to the holy ones, [32]so that I may come
to you with joy by the will of God and be re-
freshed together with you. [33]The God of peace be
with all of you.

continue

Before he can come to Rome, however, Paul has a prior commitment, one that involves the participation and generosity of several churches he founded. He needs to go to Jerusalem with the moneys he has collected for the "poor among the holy ones in Jerusalem." The impetus for this work of charity was the request, at the closing of the so-called Council of Jerusalem (Acts 15), that Paul and his Gentile converts "be mindful of the poor" among the believers there (Gal 2:10).

Paul gladly accepted this mission. Not only did it respond to a real need among the poor,

CHAPTER 16

Phoebe Commended

[1]I commend to you Phoebe our sister, who is [also] a minister of the church at Cenchreae, [2]that you may receive her in the Lord in a manner worthy of the holy ones, and help her in whatever she may need from you, for she has been a benefactor to many and to me as well.

Paul's Greetings

[3]Greet Prisca and Aquila, my co-workers in Christ Jesus, [4]who risked their necks for my life, to whom not only I am grateful but also all the churches of the Gentiles; [5]greet also the church at their house. Greet my beloved Epaenetus, who was the firstfruits in Asia for Christ. [6]Greet Mary,

continue

but it also represented for him a concrete expression of the reconciliation God had brought about in calling together the family of faith that consisted of Jews and Gentiles who truly regarded and treated one another as brothers and sisters in the Lord. Moreover, the collection was a work of justice. On the one hand, the Gentile believers were deeply indebted to the original Jewish believers and their successors for the "spiritual blessings" of the gospel; without them, the gospel would never have gone beyond the confines of Jerusalem. On the other hand, those among the Gentiles who were blessed with material abundance (see below for the comments on Gaius and other members of the church in Corinth) were now in a position to share those resources with poorer members. (For more on the collection and, especially, its linkage to God's grace, see 2 Cor 8–9.)

While Paul is determined to follow through with the work of the collection, he also has some fear and trepidation about the reception he will receive in Jerusalem. We have seen how he faced various criticisms concerning his gospel proclamation (think of some of the provocative statements he makes about the Jewish law in this letter—e.g., 3:20; 4:13; 7:7, 23; 8:3). He thus asks the community in Rome to pray for him: that he be protected from those who oppose him, that the gift from the largely Gentile churches be accepted, and that his stop in Rome on the way to Spain be fruitful. Alas, Acts 21:27-36 recounts, in part, how the apostle's fears about what could happen to him in Jerusalem were not unfounded.

16:1-2 Phoebe Commended

These two verses function as a recommendation for a woman named Phoebe. Letters of recommendation were important and necessary in the early church because of the itinerant nature of the movement, which required the extension of hospitality to people who were previously unknown. The New Testament has a number of examples of such letters (see Acts 18:27; 2 Cor 8:16-24; 3 John 12).

Paul commends Phoebe in three ways: first, as a "sister" in the family of faith; second, as a "minister" (*diakonos*, from which we get the word "deacon") of the church in Cenchreae, the eastern port of Corinth; and third, as a "benefactor" to the apostle and to other members of the Christian movement. As a sister in the faith, Phoebe deserved their welcome. As a minister or deacon, she held a position of leadership in the church. (What exactly this involved is the subject of much study and interest today in terms of women's leadership roles in the early church.) As a benefactor, she must have been a woman of means who used those means in the service of ministry (much like the women mentioned in Luke 8:2-3 who supported Jesus' ministry).

Phoebe was likely a businesswoman whom Paul entrusted with carrying his letter to the believers in Rome (as there was no general postal system). In addition to asking them to welcome her, Paul requested that they cooperate with her efforts to get the ball rolling on preparations for his mission to Spain. As the bearer of the letter, Phoebe was probably the person who read it to the community. (Most people were not literate at this time.) And as the reader of the letter, it is quite possible that she was its first interpreter, since the Romans very well may have had many of the same questions that we ask about this letter! Given that we still have and value this letter, Phoebe's mission must have been successful.

St. John Chrysostom, a 4th century father of the church known for his preaching, said this about **St. Phoebe** in a homily on Romans: "Note how many ways Paul dignifies Phoebe. He mentions her before all the rest and even calls her his sister. It is no small thing to be called the sister of Paul! Moreover, he has mentioned her rank of deacon as well." St. Phoebe's feast day is celebrated on September 3.

16:3-16 Paul's Greetings

As is often done in correspondence today, before closing his letter Paul sends a series of greetings—both to the recipients and from those who were with him. The list of people

who has worked hard for you.
7Greet Andronicus and Junia, my relatives and my fellow prisoners; they are prominent among the apostles and they were in Christ before me.
8Greet Ampliatus, my beloved in the Lord.
9Greet Urbanus, our co-worker in Christ, and my beloved Stachys.
10Greet Apelles, who is approved in Christ. Greet those who belong to the family of Aristobulus.
11Greet my relative Herodion. Greet those in the Lord who belong to the family of Narcissus.
12Greet those workers in the Lord, Tryphaena and Tryphosa. Greet the beloved Persis, who has worked hard in the Lord.
13Greet Rufus, chosen in the Lord, and his mother and mine.
14Greet Asyncritus, Phlegon, Hermes, Patrobas, Hermas, and the brothers who are with them.
15Greet Philologus, Julia, Nereus and his sister, and Olympas, and all the holy ones who are with them.
16Greet one another with a holy kiss. All the churches of Christ greet you.

continue

Paul gives Phoebe the Letter to the Romans (16:1-3).
Wood engraving after a drawing by Julius Schnorr von Carolsfeld.

whom he greets by name is impressively long, especially considering the fact that he had yet to visit Rome in person. This fact speaks to the mobility of peoples in that time. In addition to greeting a number of Paul's old friends and acquaintances, the list of people here functioned to offer to the believers in Rome a number of people who could vouch for the apostle and his work in and for the gospel.

The first persons greeted, Prisca (who is also known to us by the diminutive form of her name, Priscilla, in Acts of the Apostles) and Aquila, illustrate well the mobility at this time. A married couple, they were among the Jews who were exiled from Rome by Claudius in 49 CE (see the Introduction of this commentary). They went to Corinth, where they worked as tentmakers (Acts 18:2-3). Providentially, Paul, who shared in the same profession (as one who worked with leather, creating tents, awnings, and the like)—in his commitment to support himself when he preached the gospel—met Prisca and Aquila soon after he arrived in Corinth to proclaim the gospel. They, too, were Christ-believers and joined the apostle in his work of evangelization, as indicated by his referring to them as "co-workers." The fact that Prisca is mentioned before Aquila (also in Acts 18:18, 26; 2 Tim 4:19)—against the convention of listing the male partner first—could indicate her role of leadership in their ministry. After some time, they accompanied Paul to Ephesus, where they hosted a house church (Acts 18:18-19; see also 1 Cor 16:19). In 54 CE, when Nero became emperor, Claudius's edict was rescinded, and the couple was able to return to Rome, where they again hosted a house church (16:5).

The apostle's praise for Prisca and Aquila is extraordinarily high. Having risked their lives for Paul (we're not sure in what way), he now declares that Gentile believers owe a great debt of gratitude to them. This suggests that their work of preaching the gospel extended to Gentiles; it may also point to their welcoming the Gentiles into their house church.

It is worth pausing a moment to reflect on the important roles played by Phoebe and Prisca. Among some people today, Paul suffers from a reputation for subordinating women (see, e.g., 1 Cor 11:2-16). Undoubtedly, the apostle held many of the cultural, patriarchal biases of his time. But if actions speak louder than words, we should appreciate that Paul included women on his missionary team, gave them important roles, and valued their contributions. He thereby models inclusive ministry for the church, one that values and empowers the gifts of all.

Among those to whom the apostle sends greetings, twenty-four are called by name. By extension, even more are included, since his wording suggests greetings to members of at least five house churches (which would have included family members and slaves). Some of the people named previously shared ministry

Who were Priscilla and Aquila?

Priscilla and Aquila, a Roman couple living in exile in Corinth, learned the faith from Paul (Acts 18:1-3). This couple taught the faith to Apollos (18:26) and grew in faith with the community gathered in their home (Rom 16:3-5; 1 Cor 16:19).

Obviously, influence can be exercised in a number of ways, and this couple did so from their home. In the everyday business of their lives, they witnessed to the Gospel they had received, and, as a result, others gathered around them and formed a community of believers. They earned the trust of Paul, the great evangelist, and likewise the trust of others seeking to know the truth.

As heads of a local community of believers, Priscilla and Aquila were essential to building the church. Their mission was neither to travel as Paul did nor to preach to the masses as Apollos did, but to gather other believers and to teach what they knew and experienced.

with Paul, and a few had suffered with him in prison. The names include Gentiles (the majority) and Jews (note his use of the term "relative," which recalls his phrase "kin according to the flesh" in 9:3). About one-third of those named are women, many of whom are described as having active roles. Of particular interest is the mention of a woman named Junia in 16:7. She, along with her husband Andronicus, are described as "apostles." This is the only place in the New Testament where a woman is explicitly named an "apostle." As already noted, in Paul's understanding, an "apostle"—like himself—was a person who had encountered the risen Lord Jesus and had been given a particular mission. Note that this description also fits Mary Magdalene, as she was the one sent by the risen Christ to the Eleven to announce the good news that he was alive (Matt 28:9-10). Although Scripture does not explicitly use the term "apostle" for her, by tradition she is known as the "apostle to the apostles."

Although the church has not retained the practice of greeting one another with a "holy kiss" (16:16), a ritualized version of this greeting has survived in the **Sign of Peace** shared during the liturgy of the Mass. In this greeting we extend to one another the peace and reconciliation that flow from Christ.

16:17-20 Against Factions

Before sending greetings from those who were present with him as he dictated the letter, Paul issues a series of warnings against those whose words and behavior were divisive. It is crucial to appreciate that, for Paul, one of the most compelling witnesses—if not *the* most compelling witness—to the efficacy of the gospel was the reconciled community of faith consisting of Jews and Gentiles; of people of varying socioeconomic means; and of women and men, all of whom truly regarded one another as sisters and brothers (see Gal 3:28). Within this community, the "holy kiss" (16:16) was a formal, chaste greeting performed in public that symbolized and expressed the reconciled family of faith.

Against Factions

[17]I urge you, brothers, to watch out for those who create dissensions and obstacles, in opposition to the teaching that you learned; avoid them. [18]For such people do not serve our Lord Christ but their own appetites, and by fair and flattering speech they deceive the hearts of the innocent. [19]For while your obedience is known to all, so that I rejoice over you, I want you to be wise as to what is good, and simple as to what is evil; [20]then the God of peace will quickly crush Satan under your feet. The grace of our Lord Jesus be with you.

continue

Given this understanding of the importance of unity and reconciliation, anyone or anything that created division in the community was a real threat. We have seen how Paul reacted negatively to news that some members in Rome were casting judgment on and condemning fellow members, while still others were scorning fellow members as weak and immature (see 14:3-4). Here he warns against disobedience to his teachings, selfishness, and the use of flattery (ostensibly, for the purpose of currying favor). When we look at what the apostle rails against the most in his letters, we find that he was most perturbed by attitudes and behaviors that break down relationships (recall 1:28-30; see also Gal 5:19-26). Not all were guilty of such things, however, and the apostle recognized that the majority of believers were obedient to the ways of the gospel. Similar to Jesus, who taught his disciples to "be shrewd as serpents and simple as doves" (Matt 10:16), Paul exhorts the believers in Rome to "be wise as to what is good, and simple as to what is evil."

Notice the description of God as "the God of peace." Peace is a consequence of reconciliation. Conversely, Satan is the sower of discord and division (see, e.g., 2 Cor 2:7-11).

Greetings from Corinth

[21]Timothy, my co-worker, greets you; so do Lucius and Jason and Sosipater, my relatives. [22]I, Tertius, the writer of this letter, greet you in the Lord. [23]Gaius, who is host to me and to the whole church, greets you. Erastus, the city treasurer, and our brother Quartus greet you. [[24]]

continue

What Paul insists upon here merits further reflection. While he primarily has local churches in mind, the church as a whole is called to incarnate unity and love. Jesus' prayer the night before his death was that his disciples would be united in love so that the world would believe that God had sent him (John 17:21). We do well to keep this deep desire of Jesus at the forefront of our own prayers and our interactions with Christians of every denomination.

16:21-24 Greetings from Corinth

Having extended greetings *to* numerous members of the house churches in Rome, the apostle now sends greetings *from* those who were with him as he dictated the letter. The first person to send greetings is Timothy, a valued "co-worker" and member of the apostle's missionary team. As a young man, Timothy came highly recommended to Paul (see Acts 16:1-3). Over time, the apostle entrusted him with several important missions (see, e.g., 1 Thess 3:2; Phil 2:19; 1 Cor 4:17). He is named as co-sender of six of the canonical letters attributed to Paul (2 Corinthians, Philippians, Colossians, 1–2 Thessalonians, and Philemon), which may imply Timothy's contributions to the content of those letters. His value to the apostle is evident from the following description: "I have no one comparable to him. . . . But you know his worth, how as a child with a father he served along with me in the cause of the gospel" (Phil 2:20-22). High praise, indeed.

A few other names deserve mention. One is Gaius, a prominent member of the church in Corinth (1 Cor 1:14), who was hosting Paul as he dictated the letter. That Gaius owned a house large enough to host all the members of the Corinthian house churches speaks to his immense wealth. Another is Erastus, whom the apostle describes as "the city treasurer." Interestingly, archaeologists have discovered an inscription that dates to the first century CE that names a certain Erastus—described in the inscription as an *aedile*, one of two public officials responsible for maintaining public buildings and streets—whose benefaction paved a city square in Corinth. Given that the name is rare, many scholars contend that this Erastus is the same person from whom the apostle sent greetings. If this is true, we know of at least two very wealthy members of the church in Corinth, information that belies a simplistic stereotype of the early church as impoverished.

In 16:22, the amanuensis (scribe or secretary) Tertius emerges from the quiet of his desk to send his own greetings. Most letters in Paul's day were dictated to a professional scribe. Very few people could write, and such a service was valuable and expensive. We know from a few of the apostle's letters that, at the very end, he would take pen in hand and write a short note to authenticate the writing (see, e.g., Gal 6:11-18). Scholars debate whether the dictation was precisely word for word, but the fact that Paul signed off on them indicates that he approved of the contents.

16:25-27 Doxology

The final four verses of the letter have an interesting textual history. They are found in different places in various manuscripts (e.g., in some manuscripts, they are found at the end of Rom 14 or 15). This fact, in addition to the distinctive style of the passage, have led to the scholarly opinion that they are a later addition to the letter. If so, they still provide an appropriate conclusion to the letter—both in terms of its content and the praise to God it sounds forth at the end. Thus, this passage should be appreciated and read as part of the canonical version of the letter. The determination that the text is divinely inspired means not that it came directly from the apostle himself but that it was received and accepted as inspired by the early communities of faith in the course of hearing it read in the assembly of the eucharistic liturgy.

In terms of the content of these verses, the gospel is indeed "the proclamation" about what God has done through Jesus Christ. Even more, it is "the revelation of the mystery" that is now "made known to all nations" (including the Gentiles). "Mystery" refers here to the inclusion of the Gentiles in the family of faith (see, e.g., 11:11-24; Eph 3:4-6) and to God's covenant faithfulness in saving "all Israel" (11:25-26).

The appropriate response to the revelation of this mystery is "the obedience of faith," a phrase that forms a bracket to the letter (recall 1:5). The gospel that proclaims God's righteousness—as revealed through Jesus' faithfulness in manifesting to us God's love and authentic human existence characterized by self-giving—now empowers our response of faithfulness and obedience to this revelation of divine love. It's no wonder that the apostle concludes on a note of praise to God through Jesus, just as he did in 11:33-36! One final thing we can learn from Paul as we contemplate these final verses: Good theology should always lead to doxology, as well as to transformed lives.

Doxology

25 [Now to him who can strengthen you, according to my gospel and the proclamation of Jesus Christ, according to the revelation of the mystery kept secret for long ages 26 but now manifested through the prophetic writings and, according to the command of the eternal God, made known to all nations to bring about the obedience of faith, 27 to the only wise God, through Jesus Christ be glory forever and ever. Amen.]

Conclusion

In the Introduction, I mentioned a number of topics in Romans, many of which can speak with relevance to our contemporary context. By way of brief summary, it will be helpful to review them. What is striking is how these various themes overlap with one another, thereby creating a beautiful theological and pastoral tapestry.

Romans teaches us a lot about who God is and what God does. God's righteousness, or covenant faithfulness, is a central theme of the letter and is central to who God is and how God acts. The fact that God desires to enter into covenant relationship with a people and to form them reveals that God's love—as is the nature of love—is outward directed.

The letter contains many more descriptions of God that further describe the nature of God and God's divine covenantal love: God is kind, forbearing, patient, encouraging, and merciful—among other things. That God is just and righteous also means that God is impartial, concerned with all people and treating them fairly. God's justice, moreover, is a saving justice, tempered always by mercy. As people created in God's image, we have the privilege and responsibility of growing in these divine character traits.

Self-revelation is an impulse that is catalyzed by love. (Think of what happens when people fall in love and gradually share more and more about themselves with one another.) God has been revealed to us through the sending of Jesus and the gift of the Holy Spirit. Jesus manifests who God is by his own faithfulness and obedience to God, whom he knows as a loving *Abba*, and God's ways. Just as the Father has held nothing back in revealing divine love, so Jesus shows the extent of this love by giving his life for us on the cross. Jesus' love defeated the two great enemies of humankind, the enslaving powers of Sin and Death. In defeating them, as the new Adam, he inaugurated life in the new creation.

The power of love is the power of life, the gift of God's Spirit, who not only raised Jesus from the dead but also dwells in human hearts through baptism. The indwelling Spirit, through whom we are adopted as God's children in baptism, intercedes for us to God and empowers us to take on the family likeness, shown by imitating Jesus in his self-giving love, the love by which we live as God's covenant people, the Body of Christ. This family lives out of the effects of the saving actions of God: the forgiveness of sins and our having been justified (brought into right relationship) and reconciled with God and with one another, our fellow brothers and sisters for whom Christ died.

New possibilities now exist for those who are in Christ, possibilities that can challenge cultural norms today, just as they did in Paul's time. For instance, we exercise a freedom that is marked by loving service rather than by self-assertion and insistence on one's own "rights." We are to live in sensitivity to other people's consciences (presuming they are well-formed). Another example can be found in the church's ministry as a place for women to exercise leadership in ministry.

Confident that nothing or no one can separate us from the love of God, the Body of Christ gathers as church to give God praise and thanksgiving (the meaning of "Eucharist"!). That is when the church is most "church"—the family of faith that shows what life in the new creation can be when it is lived out (using the apostle's phrase that bookends this letter) in "the obedience of faith."

EXPLORING LESSON SIX

1. What is Paul's "priestly service" (15:16)?

2. a) What has prevented Paul from visiting the Romans (15:18-22)?

   b) Why does Paul say he is visiting the Romans now (15:23-29)?

3. How does Paul's planned mission to Jerusalem (15:25-27) reflect his understanding of Jewish and Gentile relations previously explored in Romans 9–11?

4. Why does Paul ask for the prayers of believers in Rome (15:30-33)?

5. What three words does Paul use to describe Phoebe, and what does each one tell us about her (16:1-2)?

6. What do we know about Prisca (Priscilla) and Aquila (16:3-5) from other New Testament references (Acts 18:1-3, 18, 24-26; 1 Cor 16:19; 2 Tim 4:19)?

7. a) What point does the commentary make about the inclusion of women in Paul's ministry?

   b) Which woman in particular does Paul identify as an apostle?

8. Paul makes a final exhortation toward unity in 16:17-20, echoing Jesus' desire that the community of believers be one in love (John 17:20-26). Has your study of Romans enhanced your understanding of the value of Christian unity in any way? If so, how?

9. Which theme mentioned in the Conclusion did you most enjoy learning about over the past six lessons? How can this theme from Romans continue to be part of your spiritual life and practice?

10. What did you find most valuable or meaningful from your study of Paul's Letter to the Romans? What did you find most challenging?

CLOSING PRAYER

Prayer

[T]o the only wise God, through Jesus Christ be glory forever and ever. Amen. (Rom 16:27)

O God, who in your wisdom revealed your love to us through Jesus' self-giving love on the cross, we thank you for this opportunity to study the "gospel of God" as set forth by the apostle Paul. Inspire us always to give you glory and praise, especially by our Spirit-empowered lives of love and reconciliation after the example of your Son, Christ Jesus. As our time together comes to a close, we pray for one another and for . . .

PRAYING WITH YOUR GROUP

Because we know that the Bible allows us to hear God's voice, prayer provides the context for our study and sharing. By speaking and listening to God and each other, the discussion often grows to more deeply bond us to one another and to God.

At *the beginning and end of each lesson* simple prayers are provided for individual use, and also may be used within the group setting. Most of the closing prayers provided with each lesson relate directly to a theme from that lesson and encourage you to pray together for people and events in your local community.

Of course, there are many ways to center ourselves in God's presence as we gather together in groups around the word of God. We provide some additional suggestions here knowing you and your group will make prayer a priority as part of your gathering. These are simply alternative ways to pray if your group would like to try something different from those prayers provided in the previous pages.

Conversational Prayer

This form of prayer allows for the group members to pray in their own words in a way that is not intimidating. The group leader begins with Step One, inviting all to focus on the presence of Christ among them. After a few moments of quiet, the group leader invites anyone in the group to voice a prayer or two of thanksgiving; once that is complete, then anyone who has personal intentions may pray in their own words for their needs; finally, the group prays for the needs of others.

A suggested process:
In your own words, speak simple and short prayers to allow time for others to add their voices.

Focus on one "step" at a time, not worrying about praying for everything on your mental list at once.

Step One	Visualize Christ. Welcome him. Imagine him present with you in your group. Allow time for some silence.
Step Two	Gratitude opens our hearts. Use simple words such as, "Thank you, Lord, for . . ."
Step Three	Pray for your own needs knowing that others will pray with you. Be specific and honest. Use "I" and "me" language.

Step Four	Pray for others by name, with love. You may voice your agreement ("Yes, Lord"). End with gratitude for sharing concerns.

Praying Like Ignatius

St. Ignatius Loyola, whose life and ministry are the foundation of the Jesuit community, invites us to enter into Scripture texts in order to experience the scenes, especially scenes of the gospels or other narrative parts of Scripture. Simply put, this is a method of creatively imagining the scene, viewing it from the inside, and asking God to meet you there. Most often, this is a personal form of prayer, but in a group setting, some of its elements can be helpful if you allow time for this process.

A suggested process:

- Select a scene from the chapters in the particular lesson.
- Read that scene out loud in the group, followed by some quiet time.
- Ask group members to place themselves in the scene (as a character, or as an onlooker) so that they can imagine the emotions, responses, and thinking that may have taken place. Notice the details and the tone, and imagine the interaction with the Lord that is taking place.
- Share with the group any insights that came to you in this quiet imagining.
- Allow each person in the group to thank God for some insight and to pray about some request that may have surfaced.

Sacred Reading (or Lectio Divina)

This method of prayer invites us to "listen with the ear of the heart" as St. Benedict's Rule would say. We listen to the words and the phrasing, asking God to speak to our innermost being. Again, this method of prayer is most often used in an individual setting but may also be used in an adapted way within a group.

A suggested process:

- Select a scene from the chapters in the particular lesson.
- Read the scene out loud in the group, perhaps two times.
- Ask group members to ponder a word or phrase that stands out to them.
- The group members could then simply speak the word or phrase as a kind of litany of what was meaningful for your group.
- Allow time for more silence to ponder the words that were heard, asking God to reveal to you what message you are meant to hear, how God is speaking to you.
- Follow up with spoken intentions at the close of this group time.

REFLECTING ON SCRIPTURE

Reading Scripture is an opportunity not simply to learn new information but to listen to God who loves you. Pray that the same Holy Spirit who guided the formation of Scripture will inspire you to correctly understand what you read, and empower you to make what you read a part of your life.

The inspired word of God contains layers of meaning. As you make your way through passages of Scripture, whether studying a book of the Bible or focusing on a biblical theme, you may find it helpful to ask yourself these four questions:

What does the Scripture passage say?
Read the passage slowly and reflectively. Become familiar with it. If the passage you are reading is a narrative, carefully observe the characters and the plot. Use your imagination to picture the scene or enter into it.

What does the Scripture passage mean?
Read the footnotes in your Bible and the commentary provided to help you understand what the sacred writers intended and what God wants to communicate by means of their words.

What does the Scripture passage mean to me?
Meditate on the passage. God's word is living and powerful. What is God saying to you? How does the Scripture passage apply to your life today?

What am I going to do about it?
Try to discover how God may be challenging you in this passage. An encounter with God contains a challenge to know God's will and follow it more closely in daily life. Ask the Holy Spirit to inspire not only your mind but your life with this living word.